FAITH BEYOND CHURCH WALLS

FINDING FREEDOM IN CHRIST

Dr. Dan Montgomery

Copyright © 2007, 2018 by Dr. Dan and Kate Montgomery.

All rights reserved. No part of this book may be reproduced, stored in a retrieval system, or transmitted, in any form or by any means, electronic, mechanical, photocopying, recording, or otherwise, without the prior written permission of the publisher except in the case of brief quotations embodied in critical articles and reviews.

To order: www.CompassTherapy.com

Compass Therapy® and Self Compass® are registered trademarks of Dan & Kate Montgomery.
Cover Design: David Gagne. Editing: Woodeene Koenig-Bricker. Photo: Dale O'Dell.

Published by:
Compass Works
Lulu Press

ISBN: 978-1-4303-2418-8
Printed in the United States of America

Unless otherwise noted, Scripture quotations are from the New Revised Standard Version of the Bible, copyright @ 1989 by the Division of Christian Education of the National Council of Churches of Christ in the USA. Used by permission.

Library of Congress Cataloguing-in-Publication Data
Montgomery, Dan.
Faith Beyond Church Walls: Finding Freedom in Christ/Dan Montgomery.
p.   cm.
ISBN 978-1-4303-2418-8
1. Personality—Religious aspects—Christianity. 2. Jesus Christ—Psychology. 3. Christian Discipleship. 4. Spiritual Direction.

Foreword

I've waited a long time for a book like this! Like a caring counselor in private session, Dan Montgomery writes to anyone who thinks being a Christian means conforming to someone else's pattern. To anyone turned off by squabbling among denominations. To anyone who believes his current situation is hopeless. To anyone seeking a more intimate walk with Father, Son and Holy Spirit.

    —Elizabeth Sherrill
    Roving Editor, *Guideposts Magazine*
    Author, *All the Way to Heaven*

CONTENTS

1	GOD WITH YOU	1
2	ADVENTURE IN CHRIST	7
3	A SELF COMPASS FOR FINDING YOUR WAY	19
4	YOUR HUMAN NATURE IN CHRIST	29
5	FREEDOM IN CHRIST	43
6	NATURALLY SUPERNATURAL LIFE	57
7	FAITH BEYOND CHURCH WALLS	65
8	THE DEVIL IS EMOTIONALLY DISTURBED	77
9	THE BEAUTY OF LITTLE PRAYERS	89
10	TRUSTING THE LORD HERE AND NOW	107
	APPENDIX: COMPASS THEORY IN A NUTSHELL	119

1

GOD WITH YOU

Come. Let's take a little trip. Where we're going the sun is warm on the skin. In a moment you'll see a rocky bluff, quite huge, jutting up out of a mountain landscape. Yes. There it is. See the trail next to it? It will take us right to the summit.

The woods are thick at the mountain's base. You take a whiff of the pine-scented air. It's normally a two-hour hike to the top, but we are whisked up and carried aloft like helium-filled balloons.

As we float along the trail, you notice that the trees thin out the higher we go. We drift over signs posted every several miles, but are too high up to actually read them. When we reach an altitude of several thousand feet, I point to a cave and tell you that a hermit with a long shaggy beard once lived there.

A few more seconds and we arrive at the pinnacle of the bald peak, where boulders overpower all but a few hardy trees. You step over to the cliff's edge and look down. A squiggle in your stomach lets you know it's a twenty-storey drop to the forest below. You step back for safer footing. I pick up a rock and lob it out and away. Four seconds. Then click-clack, click-clack.

You glance at me, wondering why I brought you here. What does this peak have to do with Jesus Christ?

I point south. You narrow your eyes, following my index finger to where the cobalt sky melts into gray-brown earth seventy-five miles away. "This mountain represents the journey of finding and doing God's will," I say. "The base of the mountain marks the beginning—your childhood and youth. I'm curious what those years were like for you."

You tell me about your family and friendships. What school was like. How you handled hurts and achievements. Some of your struggles.

I take two cans of soda out of a knapsack, pop the tabs, and hand you one that is cool to the touch. "Sometimes it's hard to find our way at the beginning of life," I say. "Hard to tell the forest for the trees. Christ was with you back then. Did you see him?"

You tell me whether or not you sensed God in your journey to adulthood. I listen, turning over a pebble in my hand. I always feel spellbound in hearing about a person's quest for God. I know the difficulties this quest can bring.

As you take another sip of the soda, you realize that the upper section of this mountain climb represents choices you've yet to make.

Packing our empty cans in the knapsack, I say, "Do you know who else lives here on the summit?"

"Another hermit?" you ask.

"No. It's a person who knows your name. Who thinks you're wonderful."

You remember why I am writing this book. "Christ? Here?"

I nod.

You close your eyes. A shimmer of serenity warms your heart. You're not quite sure how long you've stood there when the presence lifts. You look at me and say, "You wanted me to know that Jesus is always where I am, didn't you."

I nod. "Yes, the Lord is with you. He knows where you've been and where you're headed. He's walking with you from the base to the summit of your life's journey. Someday you'll meet him face to face."

Your shoulders relax. Like Peter, James, and John on the Mount of Transfiguration, something in you would like to stay on top of this mountain, where life feels tranquil and the view brings awe. A yellow butterfly wafts by your shoulder, then a puff of wind carries it off.

"So this peak is where I'll arrive when my journey in Christ is complete," you muse.

"That's true for both of us—and for everyone who's ever lived. The trail eventually ends. Everyone must answer to Jesus."

You take an easy breath, gazing out to the world below. Your thoughts find their way to that part of the trail you've yet to climb. How will you proceed? Live each day? Grow in Christ?

"I appreciate you trusting me enough to come up here," I say. No sooner have I spoken than we are floating effortlessly back down the trail. A startled rabbit crashes into a thicket.

You shield your eyes from the glare of the afternoon sun. We glide down to that segment of trail that is your current life.

"Remember the secret of the summit," I say, "the overview it provides."

"I'll remember," you say.

Settling in once more to where you are presently sitting, you turn over a thought in your mind like a pebble in your hand. *God is with me.* <in every situation>

God was w/ me from the time I was conceived in my mom's womb.
  He was w/ me in my past - present - + future
  - one day I will meet Christ face to face when my journey ends -

FAITH BEYOND CHURCH WALLS

2

ADVENTURE IN CHRIST

All of Christianity is rendered in two simple sentences: 1) God in Jesus Christ entered human history for a relationship with you; and 2) your relationship with Christ encompasses your personality and entire human nature.

If you took time to read a hundred theology books drawn from the two hundred denominations within Christianity, you would find a hundred different opinions on what constitutes the Christian faith. That's why I want to keep it simple.

I have led many people into personal relationships with Jesus and witnessed their surprise at his love for them. With sadness, though, I have watched some grow lukewarm later on, almost to the degree that they filled their minds with Christianese. In becoming religious they lost the adventure of walking with Christ.

I now understand that sometimes the Christian religion, while needed for presenting Christ to the world, can actually cool people's hearts toward the Lord. This shift from vital encounter to mental belief system did not occur with the disciples. They kept their personal conversations and emotional connection going with Jesus right through his resurrection, ascension into heaven, and reappearance in their inner cores by the indwelling of the Holy Spirit. Yes, they knew the same kind of fear and loneliness that you and I know. But they kept talking and praying to the Lord, entrusting him with their needs, struggles, and occasional misgivings.

So I encourage you to keep it simple. Don't get carried away with religious nitpickiness about details of the Christian life. Learn what you will and expand what you learn, but keep renewing your love for Christ by engaging him in lively conversations.

As long as you keep straight that Christianity is not Christ, and that public images of Christ are one step removed from his personal fidelity to you, you are freed from the denominational eccentricities that pervade the Body of Christ. As long as you commune daily with Jesus, you can read Scripture from Genesis to Revelation without becoming preoccupied by tangents (like self-consciously trying to obey a bunch of rules), or thrown off track by paradoxes that are not easily reconciled (like God's sovereignty and the problem of evil).

You diversify your exposure to the Christian heritage and enrich your perception of God's Being by enjoying the sensual beauty of a Catholic Mass, the rousing singing of a Baptist service, the enthusiastic celebration of a Pentecostal revival, the reverence of a Presbyterian worship service, or the relational enrichments of a home Bible study.

The World Is Your Congregation, Everyday Life Your Church

Are you beginning to see the reason for my focus on encountering Christ with your whole being and avoiding false alliances that sidetrack your responsiveness to the Lord?

You bring the self-you-are-becoming to every prayer, relationship, and situation you experience. By guarding your freedom to grow as an individual in Christ, you develop into a world-class Christian, a person who holds interpersonal communion with the Risen Lord at the center of your existence.

You rejoice that the Trinity is at work in all cultures and Christian traditions in the same generous heartfelt encounter through which the Father, Son, and Spirit relate to you. You join Peter in saying, "I truly understand that God shows no partiality, but in every nation anyone who fears him and does what is right is acceptable to him" (Acts 10:34-35). You choose not to split hairs over divisive issues or brand yourself in a manner that is off-putting to others. You concentrate on engaging the Lord and the world with an open mind, sensitive heart, and adventurous spirit.

Schisms and Hobbyhorses

Every generation of Christians struggles with religious, ethical, and cultural controversies. The Church and the name of Christ can be drawn into contemporary schisms that gnaw at your consciousness. If you don't take certain people's side in a particular controversy, you are considered a reprobate or disloyal to Christ. If you do take their side, you become an enemy to an opposing group.

Why not resist recruitment into divisive causes or movements? These only build antagonism, elitism, and paranoia—things that contaminate your simple love for Jesus. Why not serve humanity with no exclusionary clauses for enemies who don't see things your way?

If you want a cause to believe in, make it your ongoing relationship with the Trinity. That's enough to command your loyalty for a lifetime. Keep progressing up the mountain of life, remembering that Jesus entered human history for this adventure of walking and talking with you. I encourage you never to place a belief system, relationship, goal, social cause, or denominational loyalty above your unfolding adventure in Christ.

It's inevitable, though, that some well-meaning fellow Christian will try to talk you into exchanging your individual love bond with Christ for some so-called higher calling. Have you heard this before? "It's selfish to put your private spirituality ahead of the needs of our ministry." Or, "You're not a theologian. You should obey what the clergy and church officials see fit in order to follow God's will." Or, "What right do you have to follow Christ in an individual way?"

Don't be swayed. You can belong to any church, Bible study, or denominational fellowship without signing an invisible contract that says you owe them your soul. Keep your individuality in Christ: that which is most authentically you. Keep developing your personality and whole human nature, including your thoughts, feelings, senses, and spirituality. In so doing you are fulfilling Christ's desire to know and love you, and for you to know and love him.

Don't worry about occasional persecution or rejection by some groups, persons, or even institutions. Jesus knows all about such shunning. And sad to say, Christians—for all their goodness—are sometimes as gossipy, persnickety, and judgmental as anyone on Earth.

Learn to engage others without allowing anyone to emotionally blackmail you into doing their will. Seek counsel directly from Jesus on matters of deepest significance to you: "My sheep hear my voice, and I know them, and they follow me" (Jn 10:27). Cherish your individuality in Christ because the Lord himself is leading you up the mountain. *Be who I am & who God made me to Be IN HIM —*

Trust in God's Love

Now a word about how your relationship with Christ encompasses your personality and entire human nature.

Innumerable millions have known and loved Jesus Christ, both now and throughout the ages. God has made redemption through Christ so simple that even children can experience the Lord. The bottom line is that God has taken care of the sin problem afflicting humanity by allowing his Son Jesus to die on the cross in our place. It is interesting to note that among world religions and pagan philosophies, Christianity stands alone in witnessing to the Incarnation, the atonement for sin, and God's pursuit of intimacy with each person.

The Jews didn't put Christ on the cross, nor did the Romans. I put Christ on the cross. And so did you. By confessing our sins and asking for God's forgiveness, grace is imparted to us and we are redeemed. We find ourselves saying inwardly by the power of the Holy Spirit, "I am the Lord's child and God is my Papa!"

This is where the fun begins. God didn't give us the most precious gift imaginable so that we can sit on our hands, much less that we become boring religious look-alikes who spend all day trying to be good.

From the creation of humankind, God has looked for individuals to become his friends and playmates: gutsy romantic risk-takers who respond to his love for them. The next time you read the Gospels notice how much Jesus enjoyed the wedding of Cana, how transparently he comes across with Peter and the gang, how forcefully he raises his buddy Lazarus from the dead, and how sternly he rebukes the religious rule-keepers who want to make his disciples as miserable as themselves.

The Lord isn't trying to get you to copycat the lives of dead saints or act like people in the first century. He's trying to get you up and running as an original in Christ, a person who lives on the cutting edge of the twenty-first century. He wants to awaken your mind, heart, and body so that you are aware and choosing—a lively dialogue partner who brings him delight and relates to him with creative fidelity.

Nothing in regard to your human experience is beyond Christ's comprehension, nor should you hold back in shame or fear that you're not perfect enough for him. If Jesus was interested in perfection, he would have gone to another planet. Earth is in decay and turmoil. Humanity is fallen and frail. Human personality is fickle beyond belief. Altogether, it's a perfect situation for the love of God to move through redemptive hope and create wonderful outcomes for individuals who know and trust him.

Consider this. Christ as God lives at all times and all places; there is nothing within the cosmos that his presence and personality do not infuse. But there is one thing this Lord of Creation and King of Kings has never done. He has never had a relationship with you. For this he has patiently waited. Now you've arrived, and believe me, he is showing up on your behalf every day and night.

Don't worry. Christ is not invasive. He will give you plenty of room for privacy. On the other hand, he'll be thrilled whenever you include him. Have you ever invited the Lord to go with you to a movie? A dance? Walking through the mall? A workout? Have you ever chatted with him while driving around town? Or invited him into your bedroom for a nighttime visit?

The first time I went to Disneyland, I had flown to Southern California to begin a Master's program in philosophy. I was twenty-three and didn't know a single person in the state. So I invited Jesus to come along. We rode each ride in the park. Six hours later, I emerged from the Magic Kingdom, my heart pulsing with the pleasure of his company.

Harder, though, has been my handling of extended periods of loneliness, or making it through certain crises where I felt paralyzed by anxiety. There is nothing so bothersome as loneliness or anxiety, because no one can fix these inner states for us. No one can get deep down to where these feelings exist—no one except the Lord.

Christ has never removed all my emotional pain or confusion. On the other hand, whenever I've called upon him or requested guidance from the Holy Spirit, something has shifted inside me or within the circumstance that has helped me make it through. Haven't you noticed the same thing?

Even so, it wasn't until my fourth decade of Christian life that I developed the practice of calling upon the Lord throughout every single day. "Father, please help work out this problem." "Jesus, guide me through this situation." "Holy Spirit, I'm feeling afraid and really need your comfort." I still have bouts of fear or frustration. Yet I've discovered how intensely Christ loves us and how ably the Holy Spirit can impart a measure of serenity even in rough spells.

I encourage you this week to think about enhancing your adventure in Christ. Focus on making Jesus your life's organizing principle so that your relationship with him can flourish no matter what.

If you feel distracted by a situation that leaves you disheartened or sour, risk changing it. If another person has hijacked your loyalty to Christ by dominating your attention, <u>pray for the freedom to make Christ number one in your life</u>. If work, hobbies, or even family life has left you with no time for God, ask for grace to touch your heart anew.

Enjoy a spontaneous stream of lively conversations with the Lord as you climb the mountain together.

FAITH BEYOND CHURCH WALLS

3

A SELF COMPASS FOR FINDING YOUR WAY

Your personality matters to Christ. Personality is the hallmark of humanness and the gift of a loving God to each one of us. Through personality you share with Jesus the potential for identity, free choices, and intimacy with others. By engaging the Lord with your whole personality, you develop a reciprocal rhythm of communication and communion that lasts a lifetime.

I am convinced that your personality development is more treasured by God than the Milky Way galaxy, the rotation of planets in their orbits, and the entire plant and animal kingdoms. I know it's hard to believe, but Almighty God has designed Creation as a backdrop against which your personality and relationships can come to the fore in dialogue with him.

There are those who say, "You don't need to know anything about your personality to please Christ. Just read the Bible, go to church, and keep the Ten Commandments. That's what God wants from you."

Actually, these are good ideas, but only when taken alongside your personality growth in Christ. Personality is the sum total of your thoughts, feelings, and behavior. It is through understanding the workings of your inner life—your personal psychology—that you sustain a bridge of intimacy with the Lord.

Your personality is as unique as a fingerprint, yet follows laws common to humanity. Knowing and honoring the laws of personality enhances the quality of your interpersonal communication with God. Not knowing these laws, or unwittingly violating them, diminishes or even cripples your individuality and relationship with Christ.

But I have good news. There is a simple way to place these laws of personality into perspective: a personality growth tool I call the Self Compass® that is scientifically valid and biblically sound.

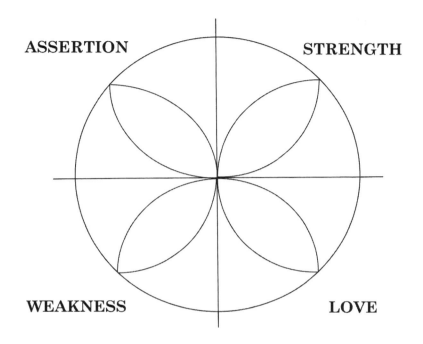

The Self Compass

The outer circle of the Self Compass symbolizes your selfhood throughout the stages of life. Resembling a physical compass, the four compass points reveal a dynamic tension between Love and Assertion, Weakness and Strength. Combining the first letter of each compass point gives you a convenient way to remember the LAWS of personality and relationships.

The compass points of Love balanced with Assertion, and Weakness balanced with Strength, are essential for a healthy personality. Yet because many people don't know this, they can favor one compass point at the expense of the others. They become "stuck" on that compass point with rigid behavioral trends that trouble them throughout life, never recognizing that many of their miseries are optional.

In overly using the love compass point, you develop the *dependent* trend of feeling unsure of yourself and always needing people's assurance and approval.

Exaggerating the assertion point creates the *aggressive* trend, where you argue frequently and feel irritated at other people because it seems that your problems are their fault.

Being stuck on the weakness compass point triggers the *withdrawn* trend of recurrent helplessness and depression. Fearful of making mistakes, you exchange the adventure of self-development for a morose existence of detached isolation.

People stuck on the strength compass point feel superior to others and become judgmental perfectionists.

This *controlling* trend makes them bossy and critical, a real pain to be around.

Part of finding your freedom in Christ is this: don't short-circuit your potential and disappoint God's calling by getting trapped in a narrow corner of your personality. Rather, live robustly and creatively with your whole Self Compass!

Here are some quick guidelines for how to get each compass point running smoothly, so you can enjoy the many benefits of compass living. For more about this, you can read *Christian Personality Theory: A Self Compass for Humanity* that is co-authored with my wife Kate.

Love and Assertion

The first polarity within the Self Compass is love and assertion. Love comes from all the times you express kindness, forgiveness, nurturance, fondness for the Lord, or sacrifice for the well-being of someone in need. Love empowers Christian service and supplants selfishness with altruistic caring.

But giving too much love to others lets them take advantage of your resources without replenishing you in return. You'll likely become a smiling doormat, a person who is secretly depressed, even resentful.

You need a healthy dose of assertion to stand up for your reasonable rights, negotiate for fairness in the world, and dare to resist others—and the devil—when pleasing them would counter your guidance from the Holy Spirit.

Think of it this way: love fosters good will and good cheer, whereas assertion cultivates self-expression and self-preservation. When you have love and assertion operating rhythmically within your personality, you can love yourself and others while enhancing your individuality in Christ. This fulfills the LAWS of personal and relational health.

For example, healthy people can say "yes" as well as "no" to requests that other people make. They can yield to others when compromise is appropriate; yet take firm stands when it isn't. Like Christ, they respond flexibly to life situations without being stuck in a trend of dependency or aggression.

A Self Compass For Finding Your Way

In the early years of my walk with Christ, I made many Catholic and Protestant friends. Jesus had told me in prayer that I would someday have a ministry to both Protestants and Catholics. But in the small town where I grew up, people generally took sides between these two great traditions of Christian faith.

On several occasions, when my Protestant friends heard of me attending a Catholic Mass or showing respect for Christ's mother, they took offense. Likewise, a few Catholic friends couldn't understand why I would go to Protestant services. They felt that my initiation into the Christian faith wasn't complete until such time as I might go through the RCIA process and be baptized a Roman Catholic.

I often stood alone. More than once I received rejection from both communities. Of course, there were a few wonderful individuals who understood and affirmed my personal pathway. I'd like to count you among them.

Maturing as an individual in Christ, then, entails learning to trust your Self Compass and follow your inner marching orders from God. Honoring the rhythm between love and assertion increases your fidelity to God's unfolding will. The Holy Spirit faithfully guides you precisely because of your courage and flexibility. Remember Jesus' promise: "I have said these things while I am still with you. But the Advocate, the Holy Spirit, whom the Father will send in my name, will teach you everything, and remind you of all that I have said to you" (Jn 14: 25-26).

Weakness and Strength

The other polarity of personality is weakness and strength. Weakness captures all the times you feel uncertain, vulnerable, anxious, hurt, sad, lonely, fatigued, stressed out, overwhelmed, frustrated, and confused. You might immediately think: "These are bad feelings. I don't ever want to feel this way." Yet Christ knows that by admitting your weaknesses and deficiencies, you are made humbly reliant on him.

For those super-person Christians who claim to be strong all the time, I say, "Why don't you grow more human, like Christ is human? He had moments of loneliness, doubt, frustration, and anguish. Are you greater than the Lord?"

A Self Compass For Finding Your Way

Owning your clay feet actually makes you more appealing to others. They feel more comfortable around you. The truth is that every person feels a rhythm between strength and weakness throughout a given day. The Self Compass simply encourages you to become aware of these normal oscillations, so that you can handle them intelligently and productively.

When artfully managed, the weakness compass point fosters humility and empathy for others who are suffering. Strength, on the other hand, imparts the confidence required to develop your talents, pursue the education you need, interview for jobs, hold your own in relationships, and feel good about your accomplishments. Understood this way, strength encompasses the occasions when you feel healthy confidence, adequacy, and esteem for yourself or others.

When you integrate weakness and strength into your relationship with Christ, you find yourself able to converse with him day and night, asking for blessing and guidance in everything you do. At the same time, you take responsibility for your choices. You do the footwork to make good things happen instead of magically hoping that life will get better.

If you combine the four compass points into a single prayer, it might go like this:

"God, please strengthen my weaknesses and help me develop humility about my strengths. Show me how to care for people assertively and maintain a caring attitude when I assert myself. Thanks. Amen."

Now I'm going to travel around the four compass points in composing my own spontaneous prayer. Want to listen in?

"Lord, please transcend my limitations and make this book effective for enriching the reader's life. Don't forget to help me pay the bills this month. And help me stay emotionally close to my wife Kate, and not get so caught up in writing that I forget her needs. I love you. Amen."

In praying just now, I suddenly became aware that I've been writing for three straight hours. I need to get home so I can ask Kate out to the movies, or maybe take her tango dancing. I don't want to make her a writing widow!

I'll see you later, when I develop the next chapter on relating to Christ with your whole human nature.

YOUR HUMAN NATURE IN CHRIST

What constitutes human nature? The question has baffled people for eons. In exploring it I want to suggest ways that your human nature can empower your individuality in Christ.

Books by theologians, philosophers, and psychologists abound with varying views about what comprises human nature. Most positions emphasize one facet of humanness as all-important. Rationalists teach that the mind is the key to understanding human nature. Romantics argue that the heart is the crucial thing. Hedonists say no, the body and its pleasures should prevail. And Gnostics say the spirit alone is real.

But why not combine all the parts that God has made in us, so we can function with a complete package? As you might expect, the compass model presents the case for holistic human nature, suggesting that since Christ, the God-person, experienced and expressed his mind and heart, body and spirit, then perhaps you and I should, too.

Your Whole Human Nature

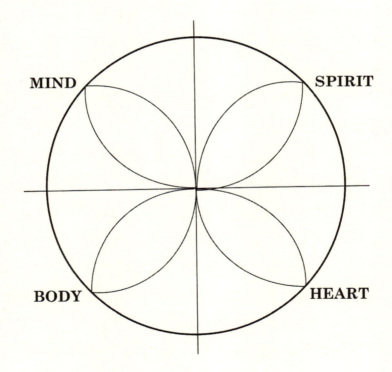

Human Nature Compass

The compass approach is intuitive. Common sense tells you that the mind is for thinking, the heart for feeling, the body for sensing, and the spirit for communing with God. Simple though it is, the human nature compass combines the sophistication of a multimodal model with the witness of Christ's human nature as revealed in the Gospels.

Jesus affirmed our human natures as he affirmed his own, because he values the whole of humanness. In fact, many Gospel stories reflect his complimentary use of a holistic human nature. Do you remember when he ran across a woman who was hemorrhaging from an embarrassing female disorder? Jesus *sensed* her touch of his robe, even though a crowd was pressing him from all sides, and in that touch she was healed. Turning to face her, he *thought* about how helping her would offend those religious folks who judged her as "unclean." Nevertheless, he *felt* compassion for her twelve years of torment. With *spiritual* authority he extended kinship to her in the family of God: "Daughter, your faith has made you well; go in peace" (Lk 8: 43-48). There is a message here. I think of it this way: when God created the cosmos, he paused to say, "It is very good." Then, in the fullness of time, God sent his son to become fully human. In taking human nature forever into the Godhead, Christ says to us: "You are my kin—I've made your human nature very good, too."

Moving Beyond the Muddle

Unfortunately, Christian convention espouses a host of phrases that muddle our understanding of human nature. You hear about the flesh versus the spirit, the new man versus the old man, the spiritual nature versus the carnal nature, the unregenerate nature versus the regenerate nature, and what-have-you. But if you stick to the human nature compass, you'll have a healthy working model based on Jesus Christ.

Jesus didn't come to redeem you on the installment plan, part now and part when you've died and gone to heaven. He has redeemed your whole being now. In Christ your human nature is made trustworthy, but only if you ask the Holy Spirit to help keep you fit and balanced. Just like a car's engine can get out of whack and need a good tune-up, you've got to take care of your human nature or it will break down.

Mind and Heart

Put in proper perspective, the mind has to do with thinking, talking, reasoning, gathering facts, setting priorities, and estimating the consequences of choices. There is an age-old bias in many cultures and religions that men are somehow better at thinking and reasoning than women. Therefore, men are somehow closer to God. I feel furious when I hear this because it is so untrue. There is no male or female in Christ (Gal 3: 28). There are only individuals who can think effectively to the degree that they exercise this function.

Sure, if you don't use your brain, it will grow as rusty as the Tin Man in the Wizard of Oz. You'll lock your keys in the car, mess up your taxes, and make idiotic choices. This has nothing to do with genes or gender. It can be remedied by practice in putting on your thinking cap and reasoning things through.

Thinking is what you do in your head—literally, the frontal cortex of the brain. Feeling is something you do in your heart. People who think too much end up emotionally detached: islands unto themselves. People who feel too much are like roller coasters, reacting emotionally to every little thing.

Christ was neither a talking head, like some verbose religious communicators, nor an emotional loose cannon, like some overly zealous followers. He had equal trust in his mind and heart. He made thoughtful choices that were infused by real emotion. He was invested in his relationships, passionate in pursuing the Father's will, and steadfast in his mission. You and I are called to develop this same inner dynamism.

While thinking helps you make wise choices, emotion is the energy of personality that brings a depth dimension to your behavior and relationships. If thinking is the melody in your life, then emotions are the chords, bass, and syncopation that lets your life swing.

As an individual in Christ, you learn how to bring the aliveness of your thoughts and feelings into prayer conversations, sharing what's on your mind and heart with God, and experiencing what Christ has to share with you conceptually and emotionally.

I encourage you to pull out the stops when it comes to communion and communication with the Lord. Try talking out loud sometimes when you're stuck in traffic or taking a walk. Of course, make sure no one hears or they'll think you're nuts. Some of my favorite prayer times are at the spa when Jesus and I are alone in the sauna.

It is erroneous to suppose that God only wants to hear from you when you are calm and rational. I suppose we get this idea from prayers recited in public settings, where dignity and decorum are required. But one-on-one communion with the Lord is enriched by emotional transparency about your ups and downs, dreams and frustrations. Full-bodied communication stirs God's heart.

Poor God, when people talk to him with no more investment than they would converse with a store clerk. And poor God, when the people in church pews sit stone-faced and comatose. I believe Christ walks out of services where people are emotionally constipated.

Kate and I have a longstanding policy of praying out loud for one another during times of need or stress. We don't do this every day, but every once in a while we go through a "walking prayer." This means that one of us will pace the floor, walking and talking to the Lord, until the real emotion behind the prayer begins to seep through. Then we will allow bodily gestures, vocal inflexions, and facial expressions to gain momentum until our whole human nature is engaged.

The responses we get from the Lord are as real as our prayers. Try it. You'll find that your mind opens, your heart warms, your body melts, and your spirit is revived.

Body and Spirit

Forget everything you've learned from the misguided dualists who teach that the body, being material, is inferior to the spirit in your walk with Christ. In Jesus, body and spirit are redeemed together. The spirit brings serenity to the body—a visceral peace that nothing outside of Christ can bring. On the other hand, the body informs the spirit with its needs for healthy sleep, nutrition, and exercise. Overly emphasizing either the body or the spirit is like saying your right leg is more important than your left leg, and then hopping on that leg for the rest of your life.

When the apostle Paul speaks of a war between the flesh and the spirit, he doesn't mean you should abandon bodily cares so that you can be a pure spirit. He means that bodily appetites have limited horizons.

The goal of life is not contained in fancy clothes, prestigious quarters, or satiating the salivary glands. The goal is to develop a mindset based on trusting in the Lord's help for physical provisions (home, food, clothing, education, health), while seeking above all else the Father's will for you. When you seek the balance of bodily health and spiritual guidance, you'll find they both contribute to a wholesome human nature.

Listen to Christ's overview: "Therefore I tell you, do not worry about your life, what you will eat or what you will drink, or about your body, what you will wear. Is not life more than food, and the body more than clothing?...But strive first for the kingdom of God and his righteousness, and all these things will be given to you as well" (Mt 6: 25; 33).

By the same token, the body is a complex machine that needs quality care. Do you have a runaway compulsion for sweets, food, alcohol, smoking, drugs, or sex? If so, Christ doesn't get on your case and carp at you to give these up, but sends the Holy Spirit to help you, like through a Twelve-Step group that specializes in breaking addictions. Thank God, you are not left alone to battle a force that is physically devastating and spiritually demoralizing.

Alcoholics Anonymous, Nicotine Anonymous, Overeaters Anonymous, and other Twelve-Step groups work wonders because they restore balance to the body and spirit. You gain a reprieve from out-of-control appetites by participating in a spiritual fellowship whose foundation is trust in God and service to others. Many of these meetings end by reciting the Lord's Prayer.

Your spirituality needs attention just like the body. Opening your spirit to God does not require being religious. It simply requires sincerity, transparency, and humility. You can ask God for these qualities and the Holy Spirit will make sure they become part of your individuality in Christ. Equally important are eating and drinking the Word of God, relating to others who know and love Christ, and helping people whenever you can.

So there you have it, a short course in understanding human nature: Mind and Heart, Body and Spirit. Taken together, these complimentary dimensions provide you with a reliable set of checks and balances for cultivating your individuality in Christ.

A Personal Touch

Now I'd like to do something unusual. I wonder if you might get up from wherever you are right now—the coffee shop chair, the living room sofa, the poolside recliner, the airplane seat, the prison cell cot, the public library, or the subway bench—and step through the page into my den.

Yes, those are pine logs in the fireplace flickering their yellow flames.

You step onto an Arabian carpet, its pattern woven in burgundy, black, and gold. Bookcases filled with multicolored books line the walls. There is a leather sofa and chair placed near where we are standing.

I say how pleased I am you've dropped in and invite you to sit on the sofa. I take a seat in the leather chair across from you. Your favorite drink is on the glass coffee table between us. You express your thanks and take a sip.

I inquire about how your day is going. You tell me what comes to mind. Then I ask if you might share a little about how you're responding so far to the ideas expressed in this book.

I listen attentively to your perspective on following Christ up the mountain of life, and some of what this means for you. Warmth and humor flow easily between us.

After you've finished sharing, I confide that what makes writing rewarding for me is precisely the creative dialogue we've just enjoyed.

Now I point to a little vial of liquid on the coffee table. "This is something I've prepared for you. If you don't mind, I'd like to dab a bit of olive oil from this vial onto my index finger and place it on your forehead. As you probably know, anointing with oil is a custom in the Bible that symbolizes the Holy Spirit flowing into one's being for blessing and comfort. I'd like to pray that this kind of well-being flows through you."

You give me the go-ahead. Closing your eyes, you feel the touch of a fingertip on your forehead, the cool moisture of the olive oil as it absorbs into your skin.

And I begin to pray: "Father, thank you for this new friend you've brought into my life. Please create a wellspring of wholeness in this person's mind and heart, body and spirit—and many evidences of your tender care in the days ahead. In Jesus' name. Amen."

When you are ready, you open your eyes and sit still for a few moments. The sap from a pine log hisses, wafting its scent your way.

"I appreciate you coming to visit me," I say, extending my hand.

You stand as we shake hands. After saying goodbye, you step through the page and peacefully carry on with your day.

FAITH BEYOND CHURCH WALLS

5

FREEDOM IN CHRIST

Freedom. An easy concept. A difficult reality.

What happens to you when you enter a relationship with Jesus Christ? Is your freedom curtailed or expanded, diminished or enhanced?

Think of it this way: freedom is merging your will with God's will, so that your life choices are augmented by the Lord's reservoir of wisdom. After all, God's been around an awfully long time. He knows how to navigate your path up the mountain, while meeting your needs along the way.

Yet many people feel squeamish about calling on God for daily guidance. "I need to take responsibility for my own choices," says one man—"I can't go running to

God for every little problem." A woman who is a very competent editor of a Christian magazine says, "It makes me feel infantile to call on God for everything. Isn't it a sign of Christian maturity for me to make my own decisions and use my own judgment?"

I respect these perspectives. There is a certain amount of truth in them. God gives us freedom of choice, and exercising that freedom develops initiative and responsibility. But what is missing from these views is the recognition that Christ loves people wisely. The Lord doesn't intend to merge your will with his to keep you immature or make you slavishly codependent. He's not interested in lording his power over you.

No, the Lord wants to guide you through a rhythm of creative interaction, the way two lifelong companions talk things over and keep each other near at heart. Jesus is interested in everything you face, just as he was with the disciples. He values when you seek his counsel in problematic areas, asking his Spirit to strengthen you. His goal is to keep you free and growing toward ever greater dimensions of psychological and spiritual wholeness. Paul has it right in Galatians 5:1—"For freedom Christ has set us free."

Think about it. At all times, and in every situation, you have freedom to pray for God's unfolding will. This doesn't undermine your identity, but strengthens it. You trust God to move inside you and within every situation so that his blessings for you are made real.

If you are prone to worry, refuse to accept this as a precondition of life. Have you ever realized that worry is optional? That worry is a choice, not a necessity? Worry is a habit of not trusting yourself and not trusting God. Worry rates the Lord as a failure when it comes to guiding you. Usually we develop the worry habit when someone has undermined our self-confidence, or when a series of reversals have made us fearful that life will never turn out okay.

Worry is not God's will for you. "But I'm afraid I'll make the wrong choice," you say. Or, "How can I tell if God is really guiding me?" You'll never have 100% certainty. Don't waste your time searching for spiritual guarantees. Just build a creative rhythm between worry and trust, weakness and strength. That works just fine.

You are not alone when it comes to worry. I worry. Kate worries. All people fret when they can't control life and make it behave. On top of that, we've all been hurt, betrayed, rejected, and had the bottom fall out. We've all experienced bitter losses and moments when life has nearly crushed us.

The way out of worry is to remember that the other side of worry—the other fork in the trail—is trusting in the Lord. Deepening your individual bond with Christ helps you bypass chronic worry by leaning on him for help. You still have to make choices, and you still have occasional doubts, but you begin to know that the Holy Spirit hovers over you like a mother watching over a child.

Fear loses its grip when you trust the Lord in real-life situations and discern the nuances of his ready help in the face of need. Over time, you develop a faith history with God that bears witness to his ingenious provisions—his sometimes subtle and sometimes dramatic interventions on your behalf. This is gratifying to Christ, "who for the joy set before him endured the cross" (Heb 12:2 NIV). Though it is amazing to comprehend, our living faith enhances Christ's joy.

There is no perfect way through life, nor is there a way of living that bypasses disappointment and adversity. But you can understand that most frustrations are merely inconvenient, not catastrophic. Over the years you evolve an encompassing trust in Christ's love, reaching out to him instinctively when you face particularly gnarly problems.

Today alone I have asked the Lord to help me pay some important bills, bless my relatives who live in another state, guide Kate and me in fulfilling our life callings, and help a friend who is undergoing surgery. I even prayed for assistance in writing this chapter.

Another part of fidelity to the Lord is openly expressing gratitude to him. You catch God being good to you, never writing off a blessing as good luck or coincidence. You praise the Lord for his faithfulness, and give him lots of heart hugs. One night a few years ago I walked through our entire house, touching and thanking Christ for everything in it: furniture, appliances, paintings, scrapbooks, computer equipment, bookcases. The works. I even touched and praised the Lord for Kate, who was in bed asleep!

Watch for God's blessings in your life this week. Catch him being good to you and let him know how you feel about it.

The Bible, the Sacraments, and Christ

How does the Bible fit in with what I'm saying about developing your freedom in Christ?

The first thing to keep in mind regarding Scripture is that the Bible is not God. The Father, Son, and Holy Spirit are God. The Bible testifies to God's love for people and God's plan of salvation through Jesus Christ.

I have read through the Bible many times and encourage you to do the same. When difficult passages have me stymied, I turn to scholarly commentaries, which have their value. Bible reading enriches you with God's perspective on human history and God's developmental style of guiding individuals. Even so, the Bible can be daunting, and some of its sections are downright confusing.

God never meant the Bible to be a substitute for his one-on-one intimacy with you. Nor did he mean for the Church's liturgy, sacraments, and clerical hierarchy to act as a substitute for the Holy Spirit who indwells you. When it gets right down to it, Christianity itself should never usurp your interpersonal communion with God.

Every individual in the Bible had to go through the same anxieties, worries, frustration, and reversals that you do. Sometimes they drew strength from a community of believers, and sometimes their walk with God went against the grain of religious conventions. Even Mary, Christ's mother, was thrust outside the rules concerning engagement and marriage when she found herself single and impregnated by the Holy Spirit.

My point is that God is larger than the Bible, the Church, and the clergy. I say this emphatically because I'm not sure you will hear it elsewhere. The Lord wants a relationship with you and has moved heaven and earth to create one.

Scripture and the Church are witnesses to the redemptive work of God in the world, but you and Christ must work out your pathway into tomorrow.

Think Interpersonally!

What, then, is the way to actualize your freedom in Christ? The key, I believe, is learning to think interpersonally about God, rather than unconsciously assuming that you're in life alone. You may feel alone and lonely sometimes; that's normal. But remember this: the Holy Trinity is in your corner, dwelling in your home, living in your body, riding in the car with you—watching over you.

Start thinking interpersonally about the Trinity. Include the Father, Son, and Holy Spirit in your emotional life and daily affairs. Call on the Lord in practical ways—I mean talk to God with gut-wrenching honesty about what's going on in your life. Good times. Bad times. In-between times. Of your own free will, build a back-and-forth communication of speaking and listening to the Trinity.

Here are some ways to prime the pump. Pray for all of your relationships. Pray for your enemies. Pray for guidance at work and in family life. Pray for your development as an individual in Christ. Pray for God's augmenting wisdom to bless every little facet of your life. Pray for God to remove rigid personality trends and replace them with life-enhancing balance. Pray for your needs and praise God in advance for his blessings. Draw near to God in love and adoration. Glorify God for the coming redemption of the world and your part in it.

Love God up for the many ways he interacts with you. Lean on God with expectant trust this year.

If you are willing, I'd like to demonstrate what I mean by leaning on God. Wherever you are right now, I'd like you to get up and walk over to the nearest wall. If you're in an airplane, walk to the restroom. If you're in prison, walk to the back of the cell. If you're in the bathtub, well—wait until you dry off. This book won't be much good sopping wet.

Now lean against the wall. I mean tilt into it at a steep enough angle that if it doesn't support you, you'll fall flat on your face. Let the feeling of trusting in the wall spread throughout your body. Notice that you can even relax while the wall is effortlessly upholding you. This physical sensation of leaning into the wall epitomizes what it means to trust the Lord with mind and heart, body and spirit. God delights in this experiential surrender to him.

Here is a prayer to help transfer your experience of leaning on the wall to leaning on the Father, Son, and Holy Spirit:

"Dear Lord, I apologize for any ways I've been holding back from you because of fear or worry. I'm going to believe that you are here with-and-for me every day. Help me trust you as genuinely as I trust this wall to hold me up. Without you I will fall flat. But with you I can do all things. I love you. Amen."

There. You've faced your worries, called upon the Lord, and delighted God's heart by leaning on him. Make this your life posture tonight, tomorrow, this week.

God's plans for you are brimming with energy. He will anoint and direct you in future situations. He will oversee the events in your life and help straighten out ruffled relationships. God knows you inside and out—genes and chromosomes, talents and deficiencies, needs and hopes—and loves you tenderly. The Lord never uses this knowledge against you, the way some people might, but inspires your intuition, infuses your dreams and daydreams, brings words of wisdom into consciousness, sculpts the flow of life situations, and converses with you like I am doing right now. "'For I know the plans I have for you,' declares the Lord, 'plans to prosper you and not to harm you, plans to give you hope and a future'" (Jer 29:11 NIV).

Keep developing your individuality in Christ. In the long haul, Jesus will fulfill those heart's desires that conform to his will for you. When life seems to go awry, ask Christ whether he has permitted an adverse situation for your transformative growth, or whether you have strayed from his plans and purposes.

To discern God's will for you, pay attention to inner and outer developments. God may change your own perspective, or he may alter unfolding circumstances. You remain focused on praying for Christ's will and the Holy Spirit's empowerment. Do the next thing that seems right. God is faithful and creative in shaping events as they move forward in time. He may use a word of knowledge or wisdom spoken to your heart by the Holy Spirit. He may quicken a passage of Scripture that you recall or read with new insight. He may bring you new information by having someone call you or causing a letter to arrive in the mail. Or he may simply give you an inner peace that says, "This is the way; walk in it" (Isa 30:21).

Your job is to pray and trust without telling God how to act. God relishes helping you through absolutely anything you face, blessing you in the process. Once you've made it through, don't forget to praise the Lord for his resourcefulness and timing. He likes that.

Course Correction

Dave found a piece of property that absolutely charmed him. He set his heart on buying it and building his dream home there. In his excitement, he forgot to ask God's guidance in the matter. A year later, after an architect had drawn up plans for the new home, the city council refused to issue a building permit. In their judgment, the square footage of the prospective home placed it too close to the edge of a hill. Dave was furious and wrote several letters criticizing the council and trying to drum up support.

When Dave confided his frustration to me, I asked if he had considered that the Lord might be blocking the permit for good reason. His eyes grew wide. He said he had never prayed about the situation, but had simply assumed that the new home was God's will because he wanted it so much.

After we prayed together, Dave stopped frantically trying to get God and the city council to do his will. He surrendered his life and the prospective home to God's will. A month later, a weekend of steady rain triggered a mudslide that took a portion of his property to the bottom of the hill, leaving him thankful he had not built a home on it.

The beauty of following the Lord is that God holds no grudges. Even when you get headstrong or make an unfortunate choice, if you ask, Christ helps pick up the pieces and sets you on the right course again. If he hadn't done this a hundred thousand times for me, I wouldn't be describing it.

Remember: there is no darkness the Father's light can't penetrate, nothing that can separate you from Christ's love, and no anxiety the Holy Spirit can't help to quell. The Lord is closer than your breath, dearer than your dearest friend—a consummate guide to the summit of your life's calling.

FAITH BEYOND CHURCH WALLS

Naturally Supernatural Life

Christianity begins with Jesus. After dying on the cross, he is raised up on the third day, his personality restored, his human faculties intact. His first recorded act is to warmly greet Mary Magdalene. Then he says, "Go and tell Peter and the boys that I'll meet them in Galilee," an especially tender sentiment since Peter had three times denied even knowing him.

Yet here is Jesus picking up the thread of friendship with Mary and Peter. By the time the month is out, Christ has met with the disciples and another four hundred people who believe in him. Though his death and resurrection have turned history upside down, he is acting like nothing out of the ordinary has happened. You'd never guess he'd been recently betrayed, interrogated, whipped, spurned, and crucified, busy as he is creating rendezvous with the individuals he loves.

Now two millennia have passed and Jesus is making rendezvous with you. He calls your name and seeks opportunities to be in touch with you. Do you hear his whisper? Can you feel his warmth?

How do you integrate this Jesus of Nazareth with your life in the 21st century? Certainly it tests your capability, since a good part of humanity now believes that science and reason are the primary means of acquiring knowledge, understanding human behavior, and explaining the universe.

If you can't analyze an issue with the tools of reasoning and the experimental method, it is assumed that your knowledge isn't reliable. After all, it is taught in public schools and colleges that the natural world is all there is. Actually, this point of view has made a worthwhile contribution to humankind by eliminating many superstitions, revealing natural laws, and improving the quality of life.

Yet for the individual in Christ, a graced awareness of heavenly power challenges the artificial distinction made in today's world between the natural and supernatural—between reason and faith. When your baby gets sick, you not only want a good doctor, you want God's help. When someone you love is dying, you want more than a prognosis of how many weeks are left, you want to bring spiritual comfort to the loved one. When your back is pinned against the wall, and a dire situation has you by the throat, you want more than rational advice, you want Almighty God to intervene and deliver you from evil!

When it comes to the well-being and fulfillment of individuals, science and rational analysis aren't enough. There is a need for something more: an inner conviction that life has purpose, an indication that someone is watching over you.

Jesus Christ is the unimpeachable witness that your life matters to God. He is the Almighty Someone who knows your coming and going, and watches over you. "For in him we live and move and have our being" (Acts 17:28). And just as the supernatural became natural for Mary and Peter, so the supernatural can become natural for you.

This world belongs to the Trinity. Far from being a Creator who wound up the universe like a cosmic watch and then abandoned it, our God interacts with us all the time.

The life of a colleague of mine, a physician, once sank to an all-time low. She got several years behind in taxes to the tune of five figures, experienced a painful divorce, lost her home, and underwent gall bladder surgery, all within the space of a year. The only thing she had left was enough reason to call upon Jesus Christ for help.

Why do I use the word "reason" here? Shouldn't I say that she had enough faith to cry out to the Lord? I use the word "reason" to emphasize that when you belong to Christ, it is reasonable and makes good scientific sense to call on him for help. No, you can't set up an empirical laboratory experiment to make God demonstrate how he cares for people and moves on their behalf. On the other hand, millions of experiments are carried out hourly in every nation as people who know the Lord petition him for help and witness his astonishing provision for their needs. For good reason they learn to trust him!

God doesn't mind scientific exploration. He invites, even empowers the understanding of nature, including the study of Homo sapiens. Yet when it comes to the well-being of persons, God moves freely by exerting his transcendent will to help people out. Without his compassionate heart at the center of things, we would all be transitory blips in a cold dark universe, where names don't matter and personalities are no more significant than tree stumps.

My physician friend knew that she was not a tree stump. She called on the Lord for help to restore a miserably broken life. Do you suppose that God held her mistakes against her and retorted, "Hey, sweetie, you asked for trouble and you got it. Now hire an attorney, an accountant, and a surgeon—and work things out the best you can. When you've finished paying them, don't forget the tithes you owe me!"

What really happened? My friend witnessed a string of healing events that extended over a five-year period. Cooperating with the grace that was offered, she acknowledged her errors of judgment and followed the Holy Spirit's lead in setting her life aright. It was difficult, but at the end of the five years she emerged debt free, with enough income to make a down payment on a home. Because of her own struggles, she developed a new empathy for her patients that several of them mentioned. I could tell that invisibly, yet perceptively, she had joined the cloud of witnesses who have walked through the valley of the shadow and found Christ an able Shepherd.

While my friend's story helps to illustrate how the Lord moves supernaturally through ordinary trials, I want to share an experience that bears witness to a miracle from God in a life-threatening emergency.

One night I was driving through a hundred-mile stretch of remote country in the midst of a winter blizzard, when the car heater broke down. It wasn't long before my feet turned to ice blocks and my breath fogged up the windshield. I crawled along at twenty miles an hour, fearful that I might drive off the road.

Shaking now from the sub-zero weather, I uttered the most unusual prayer of my life: "God, please bring heat inside the car so I don't freeze to death." A minute later a breeze started blowing gently on my feet and legs. It was piping hot air. I didn't know how God was doing it, but the whole interior of the car gradually heated up to where the fog cleared off the windshield, my bones stopped rattling, and I felt warm as toast. Thankfully, I drove the remaining distance without getting stuck in a snowbank, arriving at my destination in a fully heated car. When I checked the heater the next day it wasn't working. I took the car to a mechanic who replaced a faulty thermostat.

I don't know what your needs are right now or what pressures are threatening you. But I do know that I am in your corner, with the Father, Son, and Holy Spirit. We are cheering you on, as you and Jesus make the supernatural more natural in your life.

FAITH BEYOND CHURCH WALLS

FAITH BEYOND CHURCH WALLS

Is it possible to have faith that promotes unity with Christians of diverse traditions and openness to non-believers who hold different beliefs altogether? Compass theory suggests that a non-dogmatic faith is the wisest way to grow in Christ and witness to others without alienating them.

But—"I'm a Baptist," "I'm Roman Catholic," "I'm Calvinist," "I'm Pentecostal"—say too many Christians.

"Please," says the Father, "just witness to my presence in the world. You are my children, all. I have called you and know you by name. Seek my wisdom without a chip on your shoulder that divides my family into feuding factions. Please welcome all individuals into my household and live your faith beyond church walls."

In the big picture of Christ's redemption of humankind, your religious tradition is about as significant as whether you prefer going to the mountains or the beach, or whether you believe that cats or dogs make the best household pets.

Whatever your denominational affiliation, you are first and foremost a person who loves Christ. But when you place your Christian tradition above the gift of intimacy with God, you contribute to the fragmentation of Christianity and the senseless competition between parts of the Body of Christ.

A humbler perspective lets you say, "I am a follower of Christ," or simply, "I am a Christian." If this admission brings disparagement from anyone, then you are simply being persecuted for your witness to the Lord, not rejected because of your denominational eccentricity. Sometimes this type of persecution can't be avoided. At such times Jesus will personally comfort you. But the rest of the time, seek to be a door-opener of God's grace rather than a closed door of dogmatic religiosity.

Once in my hometown I called together a group of Christian leaders for a prayer meeting. Among them were a Methodist, Baptist, Pentecostal, Catholic, and Lutheran. "I wonder if we might become a network who get to know and trust each other," I said. "That way we can serve the Body of Christ and seek to meet people's needs, no matter what their orientation." During the next hour there arose such a disputation about brand-name loyalties that my hopes for Christian unity fell to the ground.

Eventually I channeled my passion away from banding leaders together to writing books for persons like you. This is why I value your readership so much. You are the one who is becoming the face, voice, and actions of Jesus Christ, and through his Spirit, a one-of-a-kind individual.

Keep It Simple

Believe me, God takes note of your individuation and will move to benefit both you and others. You are a signpost and heartfelt witness that Jesus is alive not dead, loving not tyrannical, adventurous not boring.

On occasion, when people are undergoing pronounced adversity concerning their health, finances, job, or relationships, you might ask if they would like to receive a prayer of blessing from you. Most people will say, "Yes, please." Whether you pray silently or aloud, or simply let them know in a card or e-mail that you have interceded to God on their behalf, they will feel less lonely and desperate because of you. They will feel a shimmer of hope that God is there for them. When God answers some of these prayers, both their faith and yours will be strengthened.

I remember during my college years a philosophy professor referred another student to me because the professor knew of my faith in Christ. Leonard asked me out for coffee and the first thing I noticed was his stuttering. Only with effort did he describe his inner torment at feeling very self-conscious around people. Only gently did I raise the possibility that God was cognizant of his difficulties, and no doubt wanted to help him develop courage in social situations. He asked how I knew these things about God's awareness and intentions. I said it was because I was describing the loving God that Jesus came into the world to reveal.

Several days later we met again. Leonard said he had been reflecting on one particular phrase I had used: "God is cognizant of your difficulties." (By the way, this is the only time I've ever used that phrase in a conversation). He desired to know more about a God who was philosophically sophisticated, yet aware of people's interior struggles. At the end of our conversation, I asked Leonard if I might say a prayer of blessing for him. He said, "Ye---ess." We bowed our heads right there in the coffee shop and I said, "Lord Jesus, please make yourself known to Leonard in a way that makes sense to him, and please calm his inner fears about speaking to people." He said, "Thanks," and we said goodbye.

Two days later he was sitting in a philosophy class taught by an outspoken atheist, when suddenly a stream of liquid love was poured into him that flowed from head to foot. As he surrendered to this love, an inner voice said, "Leonard, I am Jesus. I love you."

Over the weeks and months that followed, I noticed that Leonard was hardly stuttering in conversations. I asked him about this. He said, "I can't explain it, Dan, but Christ is replacing my old fear of people with a peace I can really feel."

Open-ended Conversations

You can have long-term conversations with acquaintances, friends, or family members who are pursuing truth from their perspective, but are not yet acquainted with Christ—respectful talks that endure over years. As long as people know you are not pushing religion, they will likely remain interested in hearing some of your faith experiences. Through this process, they will catch glimpses of Christ in you. Whether they recognize it or not, they will sense the companionship of the Holy Spirit in your enjoyment of them.

It makes all the difference that you are an individual in Christ, not a card-carrying religionist. Didn't someone who already knew Christ help you to eventually accept him? Weren't you at one time skeptical, apathetic, or antagonistic toward Christ? I was all three. I join you in thanking God for those who have shared their witness about Jesus with us in sensitive and compelling ways.

Toward Diplomacy and Civility

Every generation of Christians has its debates and controversies. Some Christians fuel their identities by attacking society at large. This engenders an unfortunate antagonism from non-Christians, who feel judged and demeaned by what they perceive as Christianity's social or political agenda. What a black eye this gives the Lord, as if dying on the cross wasn't enough.

Other Christians are so sensitized to life in a pluralistic world that they never mention faith in Christ to anyone.

"Please," pleads Jesus. "Share with people that I am real to you, that we have a relationship. You don't need to convince them of theological pet peeves. The disciples knew me, trusted me, and grew in love for me. They told people about me. Follow their lead and the Spirit will guide people to me through you."

Why not witness with diplomacy and civility about the Risen Christ, while avoiding public controversy? Why not let your faith grow deeper roots than the divisive social issues of the day?

Have you ever noticed that when a Christian position is politicized, very little is communicated about the Incarnate Christ and his passionate atonement for human sin? Let alone that the Holy Spirit blesses and guides people in entirely original ways. Or that the Father is moving in the hearts of people in all cultures and religions who respond to the light he gives them.

I think it is wiser to stay focused on what is truly unique about Christianity, on what holds true in every generation: that God has come into the world through Jesus Christ for a personal relationship with all who humbly seek to know and do his will. I know this is not as spectacular or emotionally arousing as taking a strong stand on some prescribed position, but it enables you to bring the Gospel to individuals you meet over the years, the good news about friendship with God through Christ by the power of the Holy Spirit.

Relax and Grow

Maturing in your love for Christ doesn't rely upon gaining merit badges for religious performance. Have you heard any of these comments lately? "I go to Church every Sunday." "I receive the Eucharist twice a week." "I read the Bible every day."

"Please," says the Holy Spirit, "don't trumpet your religious activities as though they make you better than someone else. I am calling all people to God's Son, Jesus. Do what strengthens you in him without bragging or drawing attention to yourself. If you want something to showcase, then display your weaknesses before me, and pray that I might lead you into greater wholeness than you presently know."

If there is a temptation that badgers every Christian, it is striving to impress God or other people with religious behavior, rather than becoming more human in Christ. I'm talking about the outward manifestations of religious life. Rituals performed. Observances kept. Causes advocated. Holiness practiced. I earnestly believe that God is more interested in your gradual and thoroughgoing transformation—your development as an individual in Christ—than in cultic practice or exterior trappings.

That said, finding a church where you can grow in Christ—a home congregation, if you will—is very important. Receiving baptism, attending worship services, singing hymns, sharing in community prayer and camaraderie, contemplating the Word of God, participating in Christian sacraments, and volunteering for service add zest to your life, while deepening your individual identity. The Holy Spirit utilizes these and other means to commune with you, providing wisdom, faith, and inspiration that imbue your life with Trinitarian intimacy.

Christ yearns for you to become an individual who encounters people beyond church walls without getting entangled in religious side issues. It is your open mind, caring heart, relaxed body, and adventurous spirit that reveal to others your trust in Christ. You express empathy for whoever suffers, listen respectfully to whoever speaks, and express feelings and values when needed.

You can become an expert teacher in Christian theology and doctrine without becoming opinionated. Just keep learning about your own foibles and shortcomings too.

When you are surrendered to God like this, the Father's love expresses itself in your transparency. Christ enriches your personality and relationships. The Holy Spirit strengthens your non-dogmatic faith with interior communion and spiritual gifts. And your individuality in the Lord burgeons and flourishes.

THE DEVIL IS EMOTIONALLY DISTURBED

I hold a private theory about the devil. I believe that he is emotionally disturbed. If you want to understand the devil, think in terms of a boaster, bully, con artist, and control freak rolled into one.

Satan is a person—yes, an individual—who thrives on loveless power and shuns the power of love. He is devoid of relational or personality health, yet nonetheless has charisma, possessing the uncanny ability to make evil appealing and wrong appear right. Haven't you run across a few people like this?

The devil personifies manipulation. If you want to grasp his modus operandi, imagine any human behavior that is rigidly stubborn, seductive, conniving, divisive, or cruel, and you'll have a snapshot of Satan. Jesus knew the devil well and said: "There is no truth in him. When he lies, he lies according to his own nature, for he is a liar and the father of lies" (Jn 8:44).

A lot of unwarranted fears about the devil are quelled by seeing him as the misguided narcissist that he is. Though Satan is cunning in the lives of those who follow his lead, he cowers when rebuked in Jesus' name. He knows the truth of John's words: "The Son of God was revealed for this purpose, to destroy the works of the devil" (1 Jn 3:8).

Of course, Hollywood movies trump up Satan's power by scripting him to hurl objects through the air and make lots of scary noises. Don't fall for it. A little old grandmother with arthritis and cataracts can send Satan packing with a few words spoken in faith from the victory of the Cross: "Get out of here you devil, in Jesus' name."

Satan departs! James, among the pillars of the early church, offers solid counsel: "Resist the devil, and he will flee from you. Draw near to God and he will draw near to you" (Jas 4:7-8).

The Devil Is Emotionally Disturbed

The differences between Christ and the devil deserve mention. Jesus is faithful and true, offering abundant life to those who follow him. He loves you and takes pleasure in leading you toward wholeness and fulfillment. Christ is a faithful and true guide up the summit that leads to everlasting life.

Satan, on the other hand, is exploitive and deceptive. He pursues a warped agenda that always lets you down. The devil resents the air you breathe and would like nothing better than to strip your personality, trash your relationships, and dump you on a garbage heap, a trophy to his egotism. And he's not without his methods: he happens to be an expert at luring people into futile lives through the behavioral reinforcement of short term gratification.

I was counseling a seventeen-year-old who suffered from depression. After helping him make some progress, I mentioned that given his history of depression, he might take care to avoid the three major poisons that are peddled to youth.

"What are they?" he asked.

"Smoking, drinking, and drugs," I said.

He flashed a worldly-wise grin. "Oh, don't worry

about me, Dr. Dan. I already smoke, drink, and use—and I'm doing just fine."

It is difficult to warn each new generation about the ever-present means of self-destruction that is available everywhere. Mostly, people have to do their own research in discovering how evil works, and how tedious or disheartening life without Christ can really get.

Paul offers a list of destructive behaviors that are as accurate today as they were two thousand years ago: "fornication, impurity, licentiousness, idolatry, sorcery, enmities, strife, jealousy, anger, quarrels, dissentions, factions, envy, drunkenness, carousing, and things like these" (Gal 5: 19-21).

Christians can and do fall prey to these attitudes and actions. For this reason, it serves us well to cultivate a lifelong habit of asking the Lord's forgiveness, and seeking the Holy Spirit's counsel in making progress toward personality and relational wholeness.

What to Do When Evil Lurks Around You

While some Christians are obsessed with the devil and demons, I don't recommend thinking much about these emotionally disturbed creatures. However, if you ever feel oppressed or bothered by a seemingly evil presence that you can't put your finger on, enter a quiet time of prayer. Begin praising Christ for his blessings in your life and his absolute mastery over the devil; then rebuke Satan face-to-face: "Satan, I bind you in the name of Jesus Christ. I command you to withdraw all influence in my life. Now Holy Spirit, please fill me with your presence. In the name of Jesus, amen."

That's all there is to it. It is Jesus who has defeated the devil and the Holy Spirit who makes Satan tremble. Scripture promises, "When the enemy comes in like a flood, the Spirit of the Lord will lift up a standard against him" (Is 59:19 NKJV).

If you are troubled by a nightmare, ask God to illuminate the meaning of your dream. Is there something you are avoiding, some choice you need to make? Or is it the devil making you fearful? Either way, I recommend placing a Bible in plain sight by your bed as a symbol that you belong to Christ alone. Pray for the Holy Spirit to fill your bedroom at night, comfort you as you go off to sleep, and exert influence in your dreams.

If someone develops a vendetta toward you, a specific intent to harm you, you know this is not from God. Pray, "Lord, help this person get hung by the noose they are hanging for me." "Christ, deliver me from this person's evil schemes and gossip." "Father, I cover myself with the blood of Christ. Thank you for protecting me and bringing about justice in this situation."

You can develop a relaxed vigilance regarding Satan, and though you stand ready to command him to desist and depart, it is wise to recognize that a fair portion of the negative tensions you experience in life are not demonic, but rather psychological in origin.

If you have needs that require clinical or pastoral counseling, I encourage you to seek out a qualified professional to help you. You may benefit from perusing the principles of personality and counseling found in my book, *Christian Counseling That Really Works*. Further, you might search out a book study that concentrates on personality transformation and relationship healing.

If you suffer from significant bouts of depression that extend over months and years, you may have a biochemical deficiency that is genetic in origin, and which will respond favorably to medication issued by a physician or psychiatrist. Don't hold back from making an appointment for evaluation. Then tell that person about your history of struggles with depression, or with periodic mood swings. Be sure and explore what you've tried that has and hasn't helped. An appropriate antidepressant or medication for bipolar disorder can be a godsend in the same way that glasses can transform nearsighted or farsighted eye conditions into 20/20 vision.

When Christian Leaders Have It Wrong

Now back to our sly friend, the devil. Some people who operate under Satan's influence are prominent members or leaders within the church.

Christ never gave carte blanche to religious leaders. While the Lord equips those he calls into ministry with the Holy Spirit and pastoral hearts, he also prophesied there would be false teachers in the church: men and women who are inwardly too stubborn or proud to be led by the Spirit. Some are troubled by severe personality conflicts they resolutely deny. Others, who are driven by the "King (or Queen) of the Universe" syndrome, crave attention through their roles as huffy big shots and self-righteous judges. The devil is perfectly at home colluding with Christian leaders who are as willful as he is.

What does Jesus say about this?

"Be wary of false preachers who smile a lot, dripping with practiced sincerity. Chances are they are out to rip you off some way or other. Don't be impressed with charisma; look for character...a genuine leader will never exploit your emotions or your pocketbook" (Mt 7:15-16, *The Message*).

If you are in a church, Bible study, or television audience that has one of these narcissists at the helm, you'll feel a gnawing discomfort that runs counter to Christ's words to you: "Peace I leave with you; my peace I give to you" (Jn 14:27). Don't hesitate to seek out another pasture.

Imagine this scene. Some uptight rule-keepers in the upper echelons of religion confront Jesus one day about the authority by which he heals people and casts out demons. Here they are all dressed up in religious garb, noses in the air, telling Jesus that since he isn't working under their particular auspices, he must be working for the devil.

The Lord snaps back, "Woe to you, you vipers. You are empty coffins filled with dead men's bones. You are like your father, the devil!"

No wonder they didn't like Jesus—he saw through their manipulative tactics just like you can.

Forsake the Devil and Live for Christ

In the big picture, it is not Satan that you or I need to fear. We need to fear our own choices. We are the ones who can resist God's will. It is we who can delude ourselves by getting caught up in trivial pursuits, or losing our personalities in the labyrinth of rigid trends like dependency, withdrawal, compulsive control, or aggression.

Let me give you an example. I grew up in a town where I was targeted as an ethnic minority. I was in twenty fistfights by the time I graduated from high school. Unfortunately, I developed an aggressive trend, partly to protect myself and partly because I felt powerful when intimidating others.

I developed enough arrogance to challenge people in traffic, cut into theatre lines, and flip people off if they annoyed me. It seemed I was too important a person to wait my turn at anything. Even though I was converted to Christ at age seventeen, my behavior at times was more akin to the devil.

In my adult years I committed myself to helping others through the profession of counseling and therapy. Yet occasionally my old aggressive persona would rear its ugly head, and the contrast between the redemptive and destructive sides of me was startling.

I remember counseling several people one afternoon, and later that night exchanging words with a driver over a parking space that I wanted. I was practically ready to fight the guy! Can you believe it? Dan Montgomery—a psychologist, a caring father and husband, a man who loved God and sought to serve humanity—getting so furious that I cursed the man out. It was pathetic, really. What an easy mark I made for Satan's influence.

Later that night, I confessed to the Lord that despite all my prayers, Bible reading, and psychological training, I still had much to learn. I cried out silently in bed, "God, please help me with my temper, my arrogance, and my self-serving ways."

I had enough sense to know I could not challenge such a rigid behavior trend alone. I talked over my dilemma with Kate. She agreed to pray with me and for me, and to be a resource for brainstorming about the difficulties of taming my temper.

A few days later the Holy Spirit moved on me, bringing to mind a practical strategy for developing public civility. First of all, the Spirit told me never to assume that my old aggressive trend was completely gone—that it was part of my history and would always be there. Second, the Spirit said that I needed to pray each day for God's help in giving me a reprieve from the impatient entitlement that could otherwise trigger an angry episode. Third, the Spirit conveyed that I could make progress by waving other drivers ahead of me instead of trying to beat them out.

That week many years ago I starting waving people ahead of me at four-way stops, allowing them to pass in front of me in congested traffic, and deferring to them when seeking a parking space. This preemptive move of blessing people instead of struggling against them often engenders smiles of appreciation. But that's not the only reason I continue. Mainly, it keeps me away from my old combativeness. Not a day goes by that I don't face the temptation to put myself ahead of others. On the other hand, the new social reflex that the Holy Spirit showed me—that of waving others ahead of me—is still working.

Why I didn't learn to be more gracious during the early years of my walk with Christ I cannot say. I can only say that he is redeeming more of my personality now, and that I am giving less heed to that emotionally deranged fellow, the devil.

THE BEAUTY OF LITTLE PRAYERS

You know how you can walk through the mall a hundred times and never get tired of finding a great sale? Or play your favorite game a thousand times and always enjoy the next one? Prayers are like this. Every prayer is a little experience in encountering God, with elements of risk and adventure. Each prayer contributes something fresh to your individuality in Christ.

Spontaneous little prayers—these admittedly small ways of interacting with God—include the Lord in your private life. Over the years you invite him into every imaginable situation. But there's something else. Little heartfelt prayers fulfill the Lord's desire for companionship with you!

Answers to prayer vary as much as blooming flowers. Some are like pansies that blossom overnight. Others are like bulbs planted in winter soil, which seem not to grow at all; then springtime comes and they erupt with life. Still others are like roses that require care over many years, but their delicate petals and distinctive fragrance make them well worth the effort.

Whether God's response is quick or seemingly takes forever, little prayers are the hallmark of your individuality in Christ.

A Little Prayer of Longing

Gwen made an appointment to see me at a college where I was teaching. A student in my Psychology of Religion course, she had met the assignments, but kept mum in class discussions.

When she arrived for the appointment, I invited her in and offered her a seat. My desk lamp cast soft light on her frowning face.

"I want to talk about something you said in class the other day," she said.

I nodded my encouragement.

"You said that God wants a real relationship with each of us. That he knows us by name. That he wants to walk and talk with us."

"Yes, I believe that's true," I said.

"Well, I have a problem. I was raised in a Christian home and went to church all my life. But I don't feel close to God. It seems like the Lord is way too big to really know about me. I feel like I'm this little grain of sand who shouldn't bother him."

"Is it like you know God loves humanity, but why would he want Gwen as his personal friend?"

"Exactly. I'm so ordinary. I'm not that good in school and half the time I feel bored in church. I'm not anything special."

"Yet you care enough about your relationship with the Lord to come here and talk about it."

"I guess so. I don't know what else to do."

When someone approaches me about finding a closer walk with God, I don't say, "Well, just read the Bible and go to church," because this answer wears thin for those who've tried it and still feel emotionally distant from God. I usually suggest that the person take a risk by initiating a conversation with God. Then I watch for how the Lord responds.

"Gwen," I said, "I wonder if you would dare to ask the Lord to come to you in a private way that you can really recognize. Something that would show that he knows you."

"You mean just talk to him?" she asked, eyebrows arching.

I nodded. "Maybe you could say a little prayer right now, just the way you are talking to me."

"Well, this feels kind of awkward, but I'll try," she said.

We bowed our heads.

After a moment of silence, she said, "God, I have felt lonely for so long. I go through all the motions of being religious, but I don't feel you in my life. Please show me that you love me. Help me know you're really there. Amen."

When I looked up, Gwen was dabbing her eyes with a Kleenex. I sensed that she was opening her heart to God in this little prayer. I wondered how Christ would answer her.

A week later there was a knock on my office door. When I opened it, there stood Gwen with a grin on her face. She handed me a bright red greeting card and said, "Go ahead and open it."

Puzzled, I flipped open the card. The printed message read, "Our friendship will last forever." Underneath, written in beautiful handwriting, were the words, "Dear Gwen, you don't know me, but the Lord told me to buy this card and send it to you. He said for you to read Isaiah 43:1. Best wishes." It was unsigned.

"This card was in my campus mailbox yesterday," Gwen explained. "I looked up the verse in Isaiah and it says, 'I have called you by name, you are mine.'"

My heart caught. "And you still don't know who sent it?"

"No. But I do know that God loves me!"

A Little Prayer of Crisis

Christ takes as much personal interest in you as he did in his disciples. Do you remember the time when Peter felt all knotted up about paying the Roman taxes? He blurted out, "Hey Lord, if we don't come up with some money, they'll toss us in jail!"

Jesus told him to go catch a fish.

I'm sure Peter was scratching his head while threading a worm on the hook. But he did as the Master said. Before long, he caught a fish.

"Okay," Peter said, holding the wiggly creature out to Jesus. "Now what?"

"Look in his mouth and pay our taxes with what you find there."

Can you imagine Peter's expression? Between the two of them, he was the expert fisherman. He'd caught and cleaned thousands of fish, and never once had loose change appeared in their innards. Despite his doubts, Peter propped open the fish's mouth and gave the creature a hearty shake. Out popped a coin that exactly covered the taxes.

What worked for Peter will work for you. Not the fish part, but going straight to the Lord when you face a baffling dilemma.

Mel, my brother-in-law and lifelong buddy, invited me out for lunch to discuss such a dilemma. "Dan, I'm in a bind. I've contracted my summer camp out to a university football team that'll arrive next Monday. I told the coach a year ago that they could use an acre on the south lot as a practice field. But I hadn't counted on the spring rains. When I went out yesterday to check on the field, the grass had grown a mile high!"

"We could try my lawn mover," I said.

"The grass is too thick and tall. The engine would burn up."

"How about renting a tractor?"

"The soil is too moist. It would leave ruts in the field."

"A scythe?"

"That would take all summer. There's just no way to get that grass cropped short in time."

"How about asking the Lord for a creative idea?"

Mel's eyes narrowed. "Right," he said, smiling. "Like, 'Hey God, could you please fix my green acre by next Monday?'"

I smiled back. My suggestion did sound naive.

We said goodbye, but the story doesn't end there. Let's allow an invisible camera to follow Mel up the winding mountain road to Western Life Camp. He is carrying groceries for the football camp into the cold storage unit, where he finds himself saying a little prayer. "Lord, if you do have an idea for cutting the grass, I'd love to hear about it."

The food packed away, Mel saunters over to the woodpile to chop some firewood. Axe raised, poised for the first strike, he hears an inner voice that says, "Okay."

"Okay what?" he thinks to himself.

"Okay, Mel," says the still small voice. "I have an idea."

Lowering the axe, he takes a seat on a nearby stump and waits attentively. A minute passes. Then he hears, "Go tell your neighbor Joe that you've got an acre of tall grass that needs clearing. Do whatever he tells you."

Mel feels torn between continuing to cut wood and doing what the voice has instructed. He wonders if Joe will think he's foolish. But an image of the football coach yelling, "Where's my field!" spurs him into action. Mel drives over and finds Joe watering a half-dozen horses at a trough.

After a short greeting Mel tells Joe about his dilemma over the acre of grass.

Joe says, "Why, that's no problem. My horses are running low on feed and I don't have time to go into town for hay. If you'll let them graze that acre, we'll all be happy."

When the football team arrived on Monday, Mel walked the coach over for a look at the field. The man knelt down and ran his palm over the perfectly manicured grass.

"This will do nicely," he said.

It isn't easy to bring something to the Lord's attention when you feel like you should solve it yourself. On the other hand, God is a genius at developing creative responses to life's perplexing crises. Like Gwen, Peter, and Mel, you can increase your resourcefulness by "casting all your care on Him, for He cares for you (1 Pet 5:7, NKJV).

A Little Prayer for Amends

Here is an example of one little prayer that waited two decades for an answer. I'll tell the story from the beginning, so you can judge how God responded to a boy's desperate prayer. I know. I was the boy.

Saturday afternoon Dr. O'Connell stood on our front porch speaking to Mom. I watched from up the street. She nodded her head. Was I in trouble?

Twelve-years-old and fairly rambunctious, I wondered if it was the Frisbee I had thrown the day before that glanced off his windshield. Dad would belt my bottom when he got home.

When Dr. O'Connell walked back across the street, Mom shouted in her unique way of rounding me up from the far corners of the neighborhood: "Dan—ny!"

Reluctantly, I heeded the call.

When I reached the porch, she smiled and said, "Son, I'm so proud of you. Dr. O'Connell just offered you a wonderful job in August. He wants you to water his roses for three weeks while he's in Europe. Of all the boys on the block he picked you."

Of course, I wanted to play, not work. "But I have Little League practice every day."

"It'll just take an hour. He'll pay you. It's really quite an honor. Dr. O'Connell's rose garden is famous in northern New Mexico." The cash sounded good. I pictured several movies with buttered popcorn.

"Okay," I said. "How do you water roses?"

"Go to his house tomorrow at noon and he'll show you. Just remember that August is the hottest season of the year. You'll have to be very conscientious."

At noon I traipsed down the long block to Dr. O'Connell's Victorian home. The house loomed three stories high. Four pine trees towered above the front yard. I wondered what the back looked like.

Dr. O'Connell met me at the door and offered a warm hello. We walked around to a huge white gate. "The key's under this brick," he said. "I keep it locked to protect the roses."

"Yes, sir," I said.

We walked through the gate into another world. Red. Orange. Yellow. Wow. A maze of trails meandered among graded tiers of railroad ties. *A jungle of roses*, I thought.

Sweetness struck my nostrils. I followed Dr. O'Connell from one circular steppingstone to another as we made our way among the roses. Each rose had a deep hole around the base for water storage.

"That's the Eiffel Tower rose," he said, pointing. I pulled down the bill of my Little League cap to cut the sun's glare. "Over there is a Tropicana—and here is Mr. Lincoln."

He studied my face. "Remember to fill each rose trough until it's about half full. The sun gets scorching hot this time of year." I fidgeted. I didn't like conversations with adults. I wanted to leave and go break in my new baseball glove.

A last glance at the trail around the garden made me wonder if it was a mile long. How long would each watering take?

As if anticipating my question, Dr. O'Connell said, "Watering the whole garden takes about an hour every other day." I cringed. But when he mentioned what he'd pay me, everything felt okay again. I could almost feel the crunchy dollar bills in my pocket. I'd be rich.

"And Danny," he said as we walked back out the gate. "Be sure not to miss any of the watering days."

"Yes sir," I said, shaking his extended hand. I trotted off to oil my baseball mitt and pound it with my fist to deepen the pocket.

Dr. O'Connell left for Europe that Monday.

I watered the plants every other day for the first week. Reading the handwritten labels attached to each stem kept my attention through the hour ordeal. Double Delight. Sutter's Gold. The Fairy. Queen Elizabeth. I'd swat flies and dodge the buzzing bumblebees.

The Beauty of Little Prayers

The second week boredom set in. On Monday I skimped a little on each flower, cutting down the overall time by about ten minutes. I thought about the batters I'd be facing that afternoon when we played the Kiwanis Cardinals. How many strikes could I pitch?

A couple of days later we played the Rotary Dukes. On Saturday it dawned on me that I had missed watering for one day, or was it two? The rose jungle felt like a fifty-pound sack of potatoes on my shoulders. I shrugged off the worry. How thirsty could they be anyhow? The holes around them were pretty deep. A little water should go a long way. When an occasional guilt feeling rippled through my belly, I'd reason, *Later...I'll go over there later.*

On Monday of the third week I came late in the afternoon, when it was cooler. The flowers looked sort of weak. Petals floated up on the water as I hosed each trough. I gave an extra amount of water to help them out.

The week passed quickly. I hurled a one-hitter against the Hilton Hornets. The next day I played second base against the Ready Kilowatts, and hit a triple, knocking in one run.

I forgot the roses entirely.

The following Monday I remembered Dr. O'Connell and the jungle of roses. I tried to recall how many days the roses had gone without water. Four? Five? I felt too frightened to go and check. Fingers of shame squeezed my stomach like a vice.

I rode my bike around town all morning. But I couldn't shake the sense of doom. In practice that afternoon I hit two batters with wild pitches. I ached with anxiety as I rode my bicycle home.

When I arrived Mom was standing on the porch wringing her hands. She looked awful. I parked my bike and walked up the steps.

"Dr. O'Connell came home today," she said. "All of his roses are dead."

I wanted to disappear from the Earth and never be heard from again. I waited for Mom to pronounce a horrible punishment. No allowance for a year. No movies. No playing with friends. She only shook her head and said in a whisper, "He was crying."

No punishment could have been worse than those words. That night a hideous feeling squirmed in my belly. I lay curled up in bed, my heart bursting with remorse. Before going to sleep, I prayed to God that I might someday make amends to Dr. O'Connell, but I knew that nothing could replace the rose garden, now a rose cemetery.

I avoided Dr. O'Connell for the next twenty years. Oh, I thought about him all right—when I saw him walking home from the college or driving in his car. But I made sure that he never saw me. Even as an adult, I hated being reminded of what I had done.

Meanwhile, I was making gradual progress in developing a more balanced personality. By twenty-nine I had become a doctor of psychology. By thirty I had published the first version of a book now called *The Self Compass: Charting Your Personality In Christ*. God had guided my life so faithfully that I had an intense passion to share my belief in Christ's transforming love.

Few people in my hometown knew about the book. I came home from California one Christmas to visit my family. The next morning I went out for breakfast. A voice from the past greeted me at my table. I looked up and there stood Mary O'Connell. Mary and I had grown up together in the neighborhood. I hadn't seen her or anyone else from the O'Connell family for years.

"May I join you?" she said.

She sat down and we chatted. Then her face turned more serious. "Did you know that Dad passed away last month?"

I felt a double sadness, not only for Mary's loss, but also for how I had avoided making amends for my wrongdoing. "I'm sorry, Mary." The old guilt flip-flopped in my belly.

"It's okay. He died very peacefully—thanks to you."

I thought I had misheard her. "Thanks to me?"

"Dad was an atheist until a few days before he passed away. Mom and I joined the Church and were baptized five years ago. Dad ignored our spiritual life. We went to church without him, but we kept praying for him to find Christ."

I leaned forward to hear every word.

"One day a professor friend at the university gave him a book that caught his attention." She paused. "It was your book about how Christ works in people's personality."

I shuffled in my seat. "What did he think of it?"

"He read it during the last three days of his life," Mary said. "That's when he changed. His last day, he led us in our first family prayer over dinner. When Mom found him after his passing, he was sitting in the den in his favorite chair. Your book was resting on his lap."

Tears flooded my vision. The Holy Spirit wrapped loving arms around Mary and me. Mary's eyes moistened, too. Then she leaned over and gave me a hug, her brown eyes sparkling.

When we had composed ourselves, she said, "Do you know what his last journal entry said?"

"What?"

She spoke gently. "He described a peace that he had never known before. He said he knew Christ's love was real."

At that moment twenty years of guilt and shame melted away. I had been unable to do it on my own, but with God's help, in a way I still find incredible, I had at last made amends to Dr. O'Connell.

10

TRUSTING THE LORD HERE AND NOW

Whatever chaos is in the world, which ever governments are in power, and whether Christianity is in or out of favor, the Father, Son, and Holy Spirit invite you to walk and talk with them every single day. Your communication with the Trinity is not contingent upon external factors, but internal ones. Your whole personality and human nature are the means of communion with God, and that communication is a spontaneous ongoing interaction.

What a pleasure.

What a mystery.

What an adventure!

In developing your individuality in Christ, you speak your mind to God, disclose feelings of every sort, and surrender your life and body to his care. The Lord, in turn, may respond by composing sentences in your mind, hugging your heart with tender care, or imparting serenity to your body, a tangible peace that calms your nervous system and melts your muscles.

As in any close bond, conversation with God sometimes sings like poetry, and other times feels uncertain and awkward. If you come to a place where God seems distant and your burden heavy, get back to the basics. Kneel at your bedside for several nights, praying for the rejuvenation of a lively faith. The Lord is right there with you. He will help remove any obstacles and rouse your awareness of the Holy Spirit's power and presence, for "we know that all things work together for good for those who love God, who are called according to his purpose" (Rom 8:28).

Dialogue Is A Two-Way Street

Because Christ took care of the sin problem in human existence, Almighty God is now your loving Papa. Whether or not you had a good relationship with your biological father doesn't matter. God the Father offers you a healthy relationship that you can learn to trust and enjoy. He cherishes your individuality and rejoices in your pursuit of intimacy with him. I remember one of the first things I ever heard God say within me: "Dan, tell people how much I love them!"

Of course, there will be occasions when you make a mistake about what you think is coming from the Lord. Don't worry. As in any relationship, misperceptions can be corrected over time.

There will be times when you'll hear the Lord correctly, and when you follow what he tells you, the results are astonishing. I once spoke at a church in Lawrence, Kansas, where I spent the night with one of the families. During dinner, I mentioned that their two-year-old daughter Julie was very cute. Her mom, Lorraine, who had just put Julie to bed for the night, pressed a hand to her chest and sighed.

"Dan, there's a problem we're facing right now that maybe you can pray about. Julie has been diagnosed with a hole in her heart. She is scheduled for surgery next Tuesday. There's a chance she won't make it." With that Lorraine buried her head in her hands. Her husband Todd looked at me with great sadness.

I felt helpless and relieved when the meal was over.

When I retired to the guest bedroom, I tried to absorb myself in reading a novel, hoping to drift off to sleep. But I couldn't get little Julie out of my mind.

As I flipped a page in the book, a distinct inner voice said, "Dan, ask the parents to bring Julie into the living room. Pray for her and she will be healed."

I tell you, it was one thing to read about miracles in the Bible. It was quite another to wrestle with my university training in science that disputed the possibility of miracles.

I'm afraid the university training won out. I kept reading the book, pretending I hadn't heard the inner voice. Five minutes later the same message floated up from somewhere inside, so clearly that I couldn't deny it. I laid the book aside. "Okay, Lord, if this is really you, then I will do what you're telling me. But what if it's just my unconscious need to help this family? I don't want to raise false hopes and make fools of you and me both."

Silence.

"I'll tell you what," I said. "I'm going to start reading my book again. If the message about Julie is from you, then bring it one more time, and I'll go and do it." The message came again. I got dressed and tiptoed down the hall, determined to be obedient, but uncomfortable about being put on the spot. I knocked gently on the couple's bedroom door. When Lorraine cracked the door open, I relayed the message exactly as I had heard it. She said that in five minutes they would bring Julie to the living room.

When we had gathered there—little Julie asleep in her mother's arms—I thought of Christ's promise that where two or more are gathered in his name, he is among them. Not knowing what else to do, I put my hand on Julie's head and prayed my first ever prayer for physical healing. "Dear God, thank you for healing Julie. In Jesus' name, amen."

When I had finished, Lorraine looked up and said, "What are we supposed to do now?"

"Follow the surgeon's orders," I said. "Do whatever he says."

A week later I was checking my e-mail when my eyes fell on one from Lorraine. I quickly opened it and read these words: "Dear Dan, I thought you'd want to know that we took Julie in for surgery on Tuesday. The surgeon took a last minute x-ray to see exactly where to operate. Then he cancelled the surgery. He called us into his office and showed us the new x-ray, saying that the hole was gone. Julie's heart is as good as new. Todd and I are praising God non-stop. Bless you for listening to him."

You Can Always Pray for God's Will

You keep your side of the God-person communication free and clear by continuously asking to know God's will and receive the strength to carry it out. You don't pray for God to do your will, but for you to fulfill his will for your life.

What matters is that you keep fresh your passion to follow Christ's unfolding plan for you, the trail he blazes up the mountain. Doing so yields an inner peace that the world can neither give nor take away.

The difference between God's memory and human memory is that God doesn't forget his promises and commitments. He is so trustworthy that he remembers every single one of your prayers. He works, albeit invisibly, in millions of moments throughout the ascent to your life's summit, overseeing your progress and enhancing your individuality.

Even when you feel upset with God, perhaps because someone you love dies, because you are sick, or because something you counted on doesn't materialize, you can share your frustration with him. The Lord is wholly mature. He is emotionally resilient, ably handling anything you disclose to him, while continuing to nurture your development.

I have known extended periods of physical pain, disabling depression, and even worse: the anguish of feeling crushed by life and not knowing where to look next. In those times I have had neither strength nor courage to offer God. So I have offered him my weakness.

What has gotten me through is not great faith, but the tiniest seed of trust you can imagine, and barely that. If you are presently in a stressful circumstance, please know that Jesus Christ is a brilliant strategist of redemptive hope. Given time, he will get you out of this difficulty and help you move forward toward your high calling in Christ. As long as you keep following the

Lord's lead, the Holy Spirit will keep teaching, counseling, and helping you—and never one minute too late!

Isn't this the way you experience the Lord? A little guidance here, a little comfort there—all mixed together with normal fears and anxieties, ordinary doubts, and the odd mind-boggling manifestation of his power.

Your journey up the mountain of life will always be facilitated by God's faithfulness—his mysterious ways of integrating your ups and downs with his empowering provision. He knows your name. You belong to him. Under his wing, you will arrive at the mountaintop, even against all odds.

Now as we approach the end of my message, I want to return to the mountain we climbed at the beginning of the book. Come join me. Step through the page and we'll revisit that trail.

Smell the pines? Hear the blue jay cawing over in that stand of ponderosas? Lifted gently off our feet, we begin floating up the mountain. This time you see a squirrel scamper off the trail into the brush. You even see a deer lift its head toward you as you pass.

Mostly you're taking in the signs posted along the way. We pause long enough for you to read each one:

GOD IS WITH YOU

JESUS KNOWS YOUR NAME.
YOU ARE HIS.

FOLLOW YOUR ADVENTURE IN CHRIST

USE YOUR SELF COMPASS: LOVE &
ASSERTION, WEAKNESS & STRENGTH

TRUST YOUR WHOLE HUMAN NATURE:
MIND & HEART, BODY & SPIRIT

PRAY LITTLE PRAYERS AND PURSUE
LIVELY CONVERSATIONS WITH THE LORD

RELAX, CLIMB, AND TRUST GOD'S
FAITHFULNESS!

As we reach the summit's rocky bluff, it comes to you that your growth in Christ will never end. Like Jesus, you will be resurrected someday and receive a splendid incorporeal body to house your individuality and human nature. Everlasting life will only enrich and deepen the compass living you've enjoyed on Earth.

Now our feet touch down at the place on the bluff where we originally shared a soda. It's a stunning view. The sky seals the earth below with the light and shadow of sun and clouds.

You can't resist tossing a pebble over the edge. Then click-clack, click-clack.

I place a hand gently on your shoulder. "I wonder if we might conclude our time together by praying for each other."

"I think I'd like that," you say. "Go ahead."

We bow our heads.

"Lord," I say, "I treasure this time we've spent together—you, the reader, and me. I praise you for being such a loving and resourceful God. Please inspire this reader's personal growth as an individual in Christ throughout the coming years. Thank you. Amen."

I listen appreciatively as you say a prayer for me.

When we open our eyes, I look at you and smile. "Dear friend," I say, "I've so enjoyed walking up this leg of the trail with you. You're welcome back anytime!"

Appendix

Compass Theory In A Nutshell

Human knowledge leapt forward when Einstein knit together the key components of the physical universe (time, matter, and energy) into his theory of relativity and gave us the memorable equation: $E = MC^2$.

While knowledge of the physical universe teaches us about nature and natural law, it doesn't show us how to know ourselves, how to find God, or how to relate effectively to others. For this we need a theory of human behavior: a theory that knits together personality, God, and interpersonal relationships.

Here is what compass theory has to offer in this regard.

The Self Compass

Just like all living organisms are formed by combining the atomic building blocks of carbon, hydrogen, nitrogen, and oxygen, so all personalities are formed by combining the human attributes of love and assertion, weakness and strength. (For the research on this, see *Compass Pscyhotheology: Where Psychology & Theology Really Meet,* by Dan & Kate Montgomery.)

It doesn't matter whether you live in New York, Rio de Janeiro, Bombay, or Beijing, and it doesn't matter whether you lived in Mesopotamia 3,000 years ago or rent a flat in Paris today. What Homo sapiens of all ages, cultures, and religions share is the need to give and receive love, diplomatically assert themselves, humbly acknowledge weaknesses, and confidently express strengths.

Now when you mess with the atomic building blocks of living organisms—disrupting the organic bonds between carbon and nitrogen, hydrogen and oxygen—the outcome is cancer and disease. There is a symptomatic breakdown of what is healthy and living into what is diseased and dying.

COMPASS THEORY IN A NUTSHELL

Likewise, when you disrupt the healthy balance of Love and Assertion, Weakness and Strength in a person's life, distress and dis-ease results. Psychological and spiritual disorders form symptoms of anxiety, depression, and alienation that disrupt personality health.

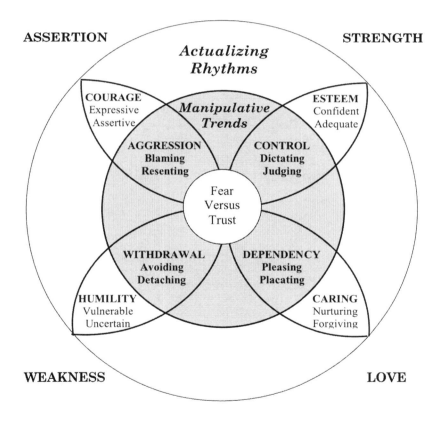

Trends Self Compass

Do you remember the Self Compass I showed you earlier in the book—the one that provided a mental snapshot of the LAWS of personality (Love, Assertion, Weakness and Strength)? Expanding this into the Trends Self Compass is like using Einstein's equation to harness nuclear energy: it provides the power to differentiate between actualizing and manipulative behavior, giving you a type of x-ray vision into your own and others' true motivations.

Healthy behavior is shown in the outermost ring, where you see the psychospiritual virtues that grace compass living. These include *courage* (Assertion), *caring* (Love), *humility* (Weakness), and *esteem* (Strength). But here's the catch. These virtues only develop when you are using the actualizing rhythms of a whole Self Compass. If you are avoiding or exaggerating one or more compass points, you lose your magnetic north and wander around in circles, following the misguided bearings of a compass that no longer works.

One-sided attitudes and behaviors constrict life and narrow options, as shown by the thicker ring tightened around the shaded area within the compass. When trapped on a compass point, a person reacts to life

Compass Theory In A Nutshell

situations in stereotypic ways that result in manipulation, or using one's self and others like pawns in the chess game of life. One repeats non-adaptive behaviors in the face of new challenges and doesn't learn from prior mistakes. Life itself loses its originality and adventure. Most of all, one loses the intellectual openness, emotional sincerity, bodily grace, and spiritual inspiration that God longs for every person to experience.

Depending upon the compass point that one unconsciously favors, one's behavior becomes rigidly *aggressive* (too much Assertion), *dependent* (too much Love), *withdrawn* (too much Weakness), or *controlling* (too much Strength)—or a combination of these. Since personality is organically related to one's openness to God and one's relationships with others, there comes to be an invisible way in which self-knowledge is curtailed, faith deteriorates from trust into fear (shown in the inner core of the Trends Self Compass), and relationships can't mature. Though it seems that something outside the self is responsible for one's inner discontent, the true cause is a rigid personality that has far-reaching consequences.

Of those who live with a manipulative agenda, Jesus asks, "What does it profit them if they gain the whole world, but lose or forfeit themselves?" (Lk 9:25).

In this regard compass theory is like Einstein's equation. It turns on the lights, makes the universe a more comprehensible place, and shifts one's orientation from manipulation to actualizing growth and development. Using a whole Self Compass harnesses the energy of personality and empowers you to relate resourcefully and creatively to self, others, and God. As soon as you see where and how you have been stuck with a fixated compass, you can take needed growth stretches into new compass points. Gradually you activate your God-given Self Compass and start locating the magnetic north of Christ's loving guidance in daily life.

Believe it or not, you already know a good deal about compass theory and self-actualization in Christ. To see this knowledge in action, let's examine a universal need for utilizing the Self Compass: raising children.

Most moms and dads quickly learn to encourage the development of compass balance in their children. You want your son to love you and share his toys with friends, but you also teach him to stand up for himself if others bully or tease him. You want your daughter to have confidence and poise, but you also teach her to learn from others and show respect.

If a child gets stuck expressing too much love, then the dependency trend sets in, which sets up the child to overly please and placate others. More assertion is needed, and you help to encourage it.

If a child gets stuck expressing too much assertion, then the aggressive trend sets in, and you get calls from the teacher saying your child is biting, hitting, and hurting other children. You counter-balance this by teaching the child to play fair, share with others, and show kindess—in a word, to love and respect people.

If a child gets stuck expressing too much weakness, you see the early warning signs of shyness, inhibition, and withdrawal into a shell. You work with this child to encourage risk-taking, the development of a "thicker skin," and a modicum of self-confidence.

If the child gets stuck expressing too much strength, you'll hear complaints from others that your child is cocky, belligerent, and bossy. You'll instinctively start teaching this child that no one likes a smart aleck, and that you don't like being talked back to.

While these four trends paint human behavior in broad strokes and are helpful for spotting and correcting common problems, you'll also be working as a parent to teach your child the art of compass living. "This situation calls for some love and caring," you'll say, whereas standing up to the class bully or the friend who is spreading hurtful rumors "calls for standing up for yourself." "Here you need to exercise a little humility," you'll coach when your child makes fun of someone with a physical disability. "And here you need to show some backbone by bucking up on your studies," when complaints about homework are aired.

What you are after in good parenting, and what you want to develop in your daily life, is enough compass balance to live creatively and responsively, rather than stereotypically and manipulatively.

The Existential Intimacy Equation

"So I'm beginning to understand how compass theory works," you say to me, "but I still don't see exactly how God fits into all of this. How do Einstein and Christ interface with me?"

Compass Theory In A Nutshell

"Wow," I say. "A powerful question. See what you think about my answer."

Compass theory asserts that physics (including the Big Bang and the theory of relativity) is not enough to explain human life in the universe, that psychology (though it is useful) is not enough to explain the meaning of personality and relationships, and that theology (though it aids in understanding God) is not enough to reveal the interpersonal nature of the Trinity.

In an attempt to bridge the gap between these disciplines, compass theory draws together psychology and theology, grounding them in the transcendent being of the Father, Son, and Holy Spirit. This approach is called compass psychotheology. And it yields an equation that connects God and people.

The existential intimacy equation shows that you are here because God created you and that the key to your fulfillment lies in freely choosing a relationship of existential intimacy with the Lord.

$$\mathbf{I}_{\text{i am}} \mathbf{AM} \rightleftarrows \mathbf{i}_{\text{I AM}} \mathbf{am}$$

While "E = MC²" makes this material world stable and predictable, it is the "I AM/ i am" equation that endows your life with loving purpose.

God revealed himself to Moses as "I Am" (Ex 3:14). Jesus used this name to call attention to his divine pre-existence (Jn 8:58). "I Am" is a shorthand abbreviation for "I Am That I Am." In other words, God is the Eternal Person (the big "I AM") from whom a human being (the little "i am") derives existence and personhood.

It's simple, really, the way God has designed human reality. God is. You are. God was here first, and has neither beginning nor end. You are here second, and your life is a parenthethical statement between birth and death. God's "I AM" carries identity, meaning, and purpose within it. Your "i am" needs God for identity, meaning, and purpose.

What does this equation say about you and God? That Christ dearly wants a loving reciprocal relationship with you: "Abide in me as I abide in you" (Jn 15:4).

Many people get this wrong about God. They either see God as an impersonal cosmic force from which you evolve and to which you'll return, or they see God's love as a one-way street in which God does everything and you do nothing.

But Jesus Christ has revealed that God is passionately concerned about whether or not you respond to him. God's "I AM-NESS" seeks out individuals who open their "i am-ness," their temporal human existence, to God's heart and companionship. "Listen," invites Jesus, "I am standing at the door, knocking; if you hear my voice and open the door, I will come in to you and eat with you, and you with me" (Rev 3:20).

The existential intimacy equation shows that God's "I AM" on the left side of the equation is always reaching out to your "i am" on the right side of the equation. When you respond to God, daring to know and love him in return, you activate a back-and-forth sharing process in which he indwells you (the I AM inside the i am), and you ground yourself in his eternal being and personality (the i am inside the I AM).

Now here's an amazing thing. Because of the dynamic power of Trinitarian love that undergirds all of creation, you can never outgive God. No matter how deeply you love the Lord, he will always surprise you with a greater provision of closeness and blessing than you've imagined possible. God backs up his invitation to intimacy with an infinite supply of creativity in loving and guiding you.

On the other hand, the unique ways you love God in return—the ways you call upon him, praise him, trust him, tell others about him—have eternal value, as Christ attests in his loving devotion to Peter, John, Lazarus, Mary, and Martha, and now you! Christ didn't die on the cross just to save you from the consequences of sin, as awesome as this redemption is; he rose again so that you can relate to him intimately every day, and beyond this life into forever. I once told this to someone who scrunched his nose and said, "Ugh, I don't want intimacy with God. I like to keep my feelings to myself." I wondered if he had unconsciously told Christ the same thing, when Jesus had knocked on the door of his heart.

$$\mathrm{I}_{\mathrm{\,i\,am}}\mathrm{AM} \rightleftarrows \mathrm{i}_{\mathrm{\,I\,AM}}\mathrm{am}$$

The two-way arrows shown in the existential intimacy equation capture the rhythm of engaging God with your whole being—Mind and Heart, Body and Spirit. You risk trusting him with everything precious, as he has trusted you with his inner life and self.

"But God doesn't need us like we need him," someone may protest. True. God exists transcendently beyond the realm of this present cosmos and the people who live on planet Earth. Yet God chooses of his own free will to invite reciprocal relationships that matter ultimately to him and profoundly impact all who enter a living relationship with him. For instance, he tells Old Testament prophet Jeremiah, "Before I formed you from the womb, I knew you intimately" (Jer 1:5 NICOT).

Because the purpose of individual life is deeply entwined with the quality of one's relationships with God and others, it's time for another equation: an equation that knits together the dynamics of identity, intimacy, and community.

The Actualizing Equation

In this universe, everything changes from moment to moment, even when that change is happening at the atomic level, and not observable by the human eye.

People change, too. An aim of compass theory is to conceptualize human change in terms of personality development and transformation, so that individuals can wisely participate in lifelong actualizing growth, rather than fixating themselves in rigid behavioral patterns.

Here we confront a paradox. Jesus, who calls us to become his friends, nevertheless gives us a commandment, reminding us that he not only loves us tenderly, but also insists on being Lord in our lives. The commandment is far-reaching, extending out over the years we've yet to live, yet immediately applies to the whole of life here and now: "'You shall love the Lord your God with all your heart, and with all your soul, and with all your mind.' This is the greatest and first commandment. And a second is like it: 'You shall love your neighbor as yourself'" (Mt 22:37-39).

This, Jesus' primary commandment, forms the basis for the actualizing equation.

$$\text{IDENTITY} \longleftrightarrow \text{INTIMACY} \longleftrightarrow \text{COMMUNITY}$$

Compass Theory In A Nutshell

This equation shows how embracing God's overall plan for you draws together the quest for authentic identity with a concern for people's well-being in the community where you live and in the world at large. You learn to relate to others much like God relates to you: with sincerity, reciprocity, and openness to intimacy (close familiarity or friendship).

Toward the world at large, including strangers and countries where people are suffering terribly, you prayerfully foster an attitude that seeks God's blessing on them and on you. Closer to home, toward people in your extended family, neighborhood, and city or town, you cultivate a caring way of interacting that intermingles self-preservation with good will, and even help when you can offer it.

Notice in this equation how the arrows move in both directions. They represent linking one's individual life with the life of others through the mediation of intimacy, that same term we used in describing existential intimacy with God.

The actualizing equation reminds you to balance your self-interest and self-expression with the needs of others and God's unfolding will. This is a delicate balancing act that requires constant adjustments.

If you don't develop enough authentic identity, then you will too easily capitulate to someone else's will for you, or else become a rubber-stamped product of some institution. Remember that Christ is your guide and role-model. He wasn't afraid to stand against undue coercion from family, friends, disciples, religion, culture, and the devil. In fact, Jesus' development of an authentic identity as the Son of God and Son of Man required a full and vigorously exercised Self Compass that didn't let anyone or anything commandeer his selfhood and inner guidance from the Holy Spirit.

This same resiliency enables you to develop your talents and capabilities, discern your emotional needs and values, follow your unique sealed orders from the Lord, stand up for yourself when required, and actualize your freedom to become a wholly developed self in Christ.

At the same time, though, and throughout the long journey up the mountain, you need to cultivate empathy, concern, and connectedness to all human beings you meet along life's way. If they are worthy of friendship, you befriend them. But if they are controllers, prima donnas, con artists, bullies, narcissists, or clinging vines, you protect yourself from their influence, even while praying that God might somehow help them.

While you are community-minded in the sense of caring about the quality of life that surrounds you, and helping others when your assistance is appropriate, you stop short of ramroding change in people's lives or playing god junior to save the world.

Do you see now the dynamic equilbrium that the actualizing equation gives you? The sense that your own life is precious to God and of genuine worth in the universe, combined with your willingness to relate to others without manipulative ploys or undue defensiveness, while still reserving the right to protect yourself if someone tries to take advantage. "So be wise as serpents and innocent as doves" (Mt 10:16).

As I close this appendix on *Compass Theory in a Nutshell*, my thoughts turn to you. I feel appreciative that you have walked this extra mile with me. I smile, thinking of how you are turning over some of these concepts in your mind like pebbles in your hand.

I wish you Godspeed in following your adventure in Christ. Know that I count you as my special friend.

THE SELF COMPASS:
Charting Your Personality In Christ
by Dr. Dan & Kate Montgomery

"Dan Montgomery's personality theory is biblically sound."
— Gordon Fee, Ph.D.
New Testament Studies
Regent College

FAITH BEYOND CHURCH WALLS:
Finding Freedom in Christ
By Dr. Dan Montgomery

"For anyone seeking intimacy with Father, Son, and Holy Spirit."
— Elizabeth Sherrill
Guideposts Magazine

ORDER MONTGOMERY BOOKS AT
www.CompassTherapy.com

CHRISTIAN COUNSELING THAT REALLY WORKS
By Dan Montgomery, Ph.D

"The twenty-five techniques alone are worth the price of the book."
— Jim Beck, Ph.D.,
Psychologist and Chair of Counseling,
Denver Seminary

COMPASS PSYCHOTHEOLOGY: WHERE PSYCHOLOGY AND THEOLOGY REALLY MEET
By Dan & Kate Montgomery

"Stunning and stimulating. Recommended as required reading for integration courses here at Fuller."
— Ray Anderson, Ph.D.
Senior Professor of Theology & Ministry
Fuller Theological Seminary

ORDER MONTGOMERY BOOKS AT
www.CompassTherapy.com